C000157420

Dr Andrew Shanks is the Canon [...] Cathedral. He is the author of *Fait[...]* *Nature of Theology* (2005), which [...] Michael Ramsey Prize 2007. His other publications include *The Other Calling: Theology, Intellectual Vocation and Truth* (2007), *'What Is Truth?': Towards a Theological Poetics* (2001) and *God and Modernity: A New and Better Way to Do Theology* (2000).

ANGLICANISM REIMAGINED

ANGLICANISM REIMAGINED

An honest Church?

ANDREW SHANKS

First published in Great Britain in 2010

Society for Promoting Christian Knowledge
36 Causton Street
London SW1P 4ST

British Library Cataloguing-in-Publication Data
A catalogue record for this book is available from the British Library

ISBN 978–0–281–06085–6

1 3 5 7 9 10 8 6 4 2

Typeset by Graphicraft Ltd., Hong Kong
Printed in Great Britain by MPG

Produced on paper from sustainable forests

Contents

Contents

1

Beyond dogma

Thank God for the challenge of atheists

The main aim of this book is to reimagine the Church, from within. But let's begin with the challenge of contemporary atheism, and what we Christians might, in a positive sense, learn from it.

Confronted with all the noise made by present-day militant atheism, part of me wants to shrink back. The debate seems so very crude! It's so loud, so remote from the proper spirit of mutual listening out of which, alone, real truth about such matters can emerge. Nevertheless, atheism serves theology as a mirror. If the atheists have misunderstood religious faith, then that may well help alert us to how believers themselves have misunderstood, and misrepresented, the essential truth-potential of their own tradition.

We need to ask ourselves, *what form of Church life would completely preclude this misunderstanding, wilful though it often is*? What would such a Church sound like? How would it present itself?

The Question

Here's Richard Dawkins in *The God Delusion*:

It is a tedious cliché (and, unlike many clichés, it isn't even true) that science concerns itself with *how* questions, but only theology is equipped to answer *why* questions. What on earth *is* a why question? Not every English sentence beginning with the word 'why' is a legitimate question. Why are unicorns hollow? Some questions simply do not deserve an answer. What is the colour of abstraction? What is the smell of hope? The fact that a question can be phrased in a grammatically correct English sentence doesn't make it meaningful, or entitle it to our serious attention. Nor, even if the question is a real one, does the fact that science cannot answer it imply that religion can.[1]

Dawkins's exhilarating contempt has the straw man ablaze in an instant; the flames crackle. (They smell, ambiguously, of burning hope!)

But hang on a moment. I don't think theology is definable as being concerned with why questions *in general*.

It's concerned at heart with just one, very simple to ask, why question; or with one particular level of questioning 'why'. This may be formulated in many different ways. In the first instance, it encompasses the questions, 'Why am I what I am? Why do I do what I do? Why are we what we are? Why do we do what we do?' One may venture answers framed in biological terms, biographically, historically, sociologically, psychotherapeutically, philosophically. But it's where there's also a certain undertone of self-critical exasperation in the asking that this 'why?' may become religious. And then it also flows into 'what' questions, 'who' questions, 'how' questions. 'Why like this? Isn't there a wiser way to live? Is this, really, what I'm "meant" or we're "meant" to be and do? What am I, what should I be, living for? Who am I, at the deepest level? How should I be living?'

And moreover, again, Dawkins misses the point: good theology doesn't exactly seek to *give answers* here. Rather, good theology is a devising of imaginative strategies *to intensify the enquiry*.

For this isn't a form of questioning like any other. These questions are very simple to ask. They occur, in some way, to everyone. But, at the same time, the underlying question-impulse they express is peculiarly difficult to stay with. We seek to evade it. And one prime strategy for evading it is to muddle it up with other forms of questioning that are less troublesome. Let's call this uncomfortable impulse the 'Question' with a capital Q, in order to distinguish it from all the other questions behind which it may be concealed.

The 'Question' in this sense is inexhaustible. It's the *infinite* questioning that arises as soon as we cease simply to take the course of our lives for granted; it's the calling into question of our whole lives. All other questions are finite: at the end of the line, they have answers, to which we draw closer. This one doesn't. On the contrary, it's forever taking us away from the answers we thought we had. The exasperation in it is constantly at work, dissolving mere moral prejudice of every kind. As a theologian, I'm inclined to call this the caustic agency of divine grace. It's what loosens the gunge by which the soul's passages are clogged. And good theology, in my view, is the thinking that belongs to a community-building project essentially designed to maximize people's exposure to it.

What I'm calling the 'Question' – the infinite, in the sense of infinitely disturbing, Question – is everything that springs direct from the injunction: 'know yourself'. Surely, the more intensely we ask it, the better. If we don't ask it, we'll do no more than drift through life, part of the human herd. Or perhaps: part of a human hunting pack, subsumed into a war machine.

There's a scene in Tolstoy's *War and Peace* that's always stuck in my memory. Prince Andrei Bolkonsky, leading a charge at the battle of Austerlitz, has been hit by a cannon ball. Lying flat on his back, and face to face with eternity, he experiences an epiphany; suddenly, he finds himself lifted right out of the drift of life. Then – a little while later, flush with triumph, Napoleon rides by:

'That's a fine death!' said Napoleon, looking down at Bolkonsky. Prince Andrei grasped that this was said of him, and that it was Napoleon saying it. He heard the speaker addressed as *Sire*. But he heard the words as he might have heard the buzzing of a fly. Not only did they not interest him – they made no impression on him, and were immediately forgotten. There was a burning pain in his head; he felt that his life-blood was ebbing away, and he saw far above him the remote, eternal heavens. He knew it was Napoleon – his hero – but at that moment Napoleon seemed to him such a small, insignificant creature compared with what was passing now between his own soul and that lofty, limitless firmament with the clouds flying over it. It meant nothing to him at that moment who might be standing over him, or what was said of him: he was only glad that people were standing near, and his only desire was that these people should help him and bring him back to life, which seemed to him so beautiful now that he had learned to see it differently.

He groans; hearing which, Napoleon gives instructions that he should be taken to a dressing-station.

Slipping in and out of consciousness, over the following hours Prince Andrei continues to reflect:

> Nothing, nothing [he says to himself] is certain, except the un-importance of everything within my comprehension and the grandeur of something incomprehensible but all-important . . .[2]

What *is* this 'something incomprehensible but all-important' that he's encountered here? He thinks of his sister's conventional piety – to what extent is it the 'God' of that piety? It both is and isn't. But – one might say – *it's just what speaks to us through the Question, and what the Question opens towards*. It's all the energy infusing that challenge, for him now, with infinite urgency.

Indeed, the whole novel is an epic parade of characters, all of whom Tolstoy presents to us essentially in the light of the Question. Tolstoy's unique greatness as a novelist, I think, lies in the singularly direct, yet down to earth, way he does this, with such a large and diverse cast of characters. But to some extent all serious novels do the same. The special truth-potential of the novel, as an art form, lies in its capacity to present us with the Question at work. And to show us the harmful consequences of its being suppressed.

Not everyone, however, reads serious novels. Ideally we need a whole social ethos in which the asking of the Question, even at its most disturbing, is honoured and encouraged. And novels can't do the job alone. This is why we need theology: to devise forms of organization that are capable of integrating into a single coherent conversation process, energizing the Question, *all different classes of people*. For, after all, the power of the Question largely depends upon our registering the sheer otherness of other people: why am I what I am, why do I do what I do, when others are so different, and live so differently? This is what opens up the Question, in its primary form, empowers it to open us up. And good theology, then, tackles the secondary question, what sort of community life is best able to amplify that primary disturbance, by bringing the very widest possible variety of people, most intimately, together? How might we best rework our religious traditions to help promote, and create a context for, this sort of (what one might call) *soul-shaping* conversation?

Dawkins for his part expresses the utmost contempt for theology in general. He considers it to be, by nature, a sheer enemy to natural science. But this is because he's confused two altogether different species of truth.

Thus: on the one hand, there's the species of truth proper to natural science, and to all projects aiming at the explanation of objective reality, purely and simply as such. Let's call this 'truth-as-correctness'. Such truth is the ideal property of theoretical propositions considered in themselves: that's to say, *in abstraction from conversational context*. Truth-as-correctness is what counts as true quite regardless of who's speaking, or to whom: it's the truth of factually accurate descriptions and good logic.

But then, on the other hand, there's the species of truth proper to theology, and to other forms of religious thought, including for instance the non-theistic intellectual disciplines of Buddhism. Let's call this 'truth-as-openness'.[3] Here we have the sort of truth that's intrinsic to the workings of the Question: it's what a proper attention to the Question opens up, the more intensively asked the better. Unlike truth-as-correctness, therefore, truth-as-openness isn't a property of propositions considered in themselves, abstracted from conversational context. *On the contrary, it's a property of insights made manifest, essentially, in a person's fundamental capacity for empathetic engagement in soul-shaping conversation.* It's a quality of character; and, then, it belongs to everything said that expresses that quality. 'I am the way, and the truth, and the life,' says Jesus (John 14.6). The 'truth' that Jesus definitively represents to us Christians isn't just the truth of a correct theory as such – what sense, indeed, does it make to speak of anyone *embodying* a correct theory? No, what Jesus embodies is the 'way' of God's love, and hence the 'life' of the most lively encounter with other people, the most open encounter, at the deepest, most thought-provoking level. And *this* is the truth to which, in principle, Christian theology is dedicated, as a devising of strategy for its cultivation.

So, take the elementary theological proposition: 'This world is the creation of God.' Is it true or false? The proper theological answer is surely that everything here depends upon the conversational context, who's speaking, where and when.

Suppose that two people are in perfect agreement as to the purely doctrinal usage of the word 'God', but that one of them is a true saint and the other a psychopathic religious bigot. Then I'd say that – notwithstanding their superficial appearance of being in agreement – in the mouth of the former the affirmation 'This world is the creation of God' is profoundly true, but in the mouth of the latter the same affirmation is no less profoundly false. Nothing's changed in the wording or in the abstract theoretical interpretation of the words. Yet, the *lived* meaning of the statement is, nevertheless, altogether different in the two cases: in the case of the saint, it's an endorsement of sanctity; in the case of the bigot, it's an endorsement of bigotry. And that's what counts. The truth of religious propositions doesn't inhere in the propositions alone. It emerges through their actual use, as intensifiers of the Question, through a thoughtful practice of prayer. Theology has to clarify that existential truth. Everything here depends upon clearly differentiating true faith, in itself, from the dogma that's designed to communicate it to the widest possible constituency; the accuracy of the communication entirely depends upon the continuing clarity of that differentiation. As a theologian, I take it to be my basic task – not merely to transmit, defend and logically refine received dogma – but critically to consider how it relates to the transcendent reality of faith, as a matter of practice.

Dawkins scornfully refers to religious faith as 'belief without evidence'.[4] That certainly isn't how I'd define it! Actually, I think there's a problem with the English word 'belief', in this context.[5] It's ambiguous: when we speak of 'believing in' a person, this has a completely different flavour from talk of 'believing in' either a theory or an opinion. The former idea still carries traces of the etymological origin of the word 'belief', which is connected with 'love' – as in the German for 'love', *Liebe*. (*Belieben* means 'liking' or 'choice'). In the Creed, 'I believe' is of course the traditional translation of the Latin, *credo*, and *credo* has the etymological connotation of 'I give my heart'. But it seems to me that the English translation of the Creed has nowadays become somewhat problematic, because of the way in which the phrase 'I believe', or 'We believe', has become increasingly contaminated with the quite different notion of 'believing in' either a theory or an opinion. Perhaps we should therefore retranslate '*Credo in . . .*' at the beginning of the Creed not as 'I believe in . . .' but as 'I put my trust in . . .' For, faith *isn't* a theory.[6] It *isn't* an opinion, bidding for definitive truth-as-correctness; it's a 'gift of the heart', a self-surrender to the intransigent demands of perfect truth-as-openness, a prayerful process of opening up to, and being opened up by the Question.

Faith, for theology, is what 'saves' us. But, whatever 'salvation' means in practice, it certainly can't be accomplished by the mere holding of a correct set of opinions. We're saved by faith, St Paul argues, not by good works, in the sense of a correct observance of Torah regulations. And in the same way it might surely also be said that we're saved by faith, not by 'correct' belief, in the sense of a theory.

Indeed, 'believing in' God isn't like 'believing in' either a theory or an opinion, at all; it's a form of 'believing in' a person, a conversational opening up. That's what it signifies when we address God in personal terms. God in Christ calls us, personally, towards ever greater truth-as-openness. And Christian faith, in principle, is nothing other than the proper registering of that call. It's the will to respond positively: opening up towards the Question, with God recognized as the Questioner, and so trusting the divine Questioner as to drop all one's defences against the questioning.

Understood in this way, faith *isn't* 'belief without evidence'. The evidence it rests on differs from the sort of evidence that would be needed if faith were a sort of theory or opinion – but, in fact, it's all around us. Wherever one sees, or feels in one's own self, the life-transforming – because soul-opening – effect of the Question being asked with real intensity, there the evidence is. And how can any truly thoughtful person doubt the desirability of such openness? One may debate the strategic effectiveness of particular forms of religious faith for helping promote it. But *that's* surely the real issue here: how such openness is most effectively to be promoted, by poetic and organizational means. Insofar as any form of religion can help, in any way, it must be welcome. From this point of view, to renounce all religion en bloc really does seem a rather odd sort of closed-minded attitude. It's a bit like deciding that, in view of all the lies – some of them so large scale and destructive – that have been perpetrated in the English language down the ages, one had better give up speaking English altogether.

Religious dogma is best regarded, not so much as a theoretical claim in rivalry with the theoretical claims of natural science but more as a sort of grammar.

True, a lot of religion is also very closed-minded. Of course! And where it's closed-minded, its adherents do tend to be just as confused between truth-as-openness and truth-as-correctness as is Dawkins. Then indeed they misinterpret their faith tradition as a set of theoretical correctness claims. But this is what I'd call the reduction of theology to '*metaphysics*'. By 'metaphysics', here, I mean talk about God (no matter how crude or sophisticated) effectively cut loose from the imperatives of openness, and so from true prayer. I by no means want to defend religious metaphysics against Dawkins's critique. All I want to do, as a Christian theologian, is insist on the radical otherness of true theology from any sort of metaphysics in this sense. Religious metaphysics sets out to justify a set of answers to finite questions regarding the ultimate constitution of reality; true theology, very differently, seeks poetic and organizational ways to open up the infinite Question, beyond all such answers. It's none other than a struggle to separate out that Question, in itself, from all the other, lesser questions that have been thrown up around it, by way of immediate distraction. True theology treats dogma as grammar, not metaphysical theory. That's to say, it aims not at any chimaera of perfect metaphysical correctness but simply at a prayerful cultivation of ever-greater conversational generosity, in opening towards the Question.

I see no reason why theology shouldn't be just as rational, and in its own way just as rigorous, an enterprise as natural science. *All that's required is that the proper truth-criteria be recognized.*

'How I envy you . . .'

Dawkins doesn't only scorn theology. He also scorns scientists like Stephen Jay Gould who, although not a religious man himself, nevertheless appreciated the ultimate non-rivalry of science and religion. He quotes Gould:

> The net, or magisterium, of science covers the empirical realm: what is the universe made of (fact) and why does it work this way (theory). The magisterium of religion extends over questions of ultimate meaning and moral value. These two magisteria do not overlap, nor do they encompass all enquiry (consider, for example, the magisterium of art and the meaning of beauty). To cite the old clichés, science gets the age of rocks, and religion the rock of ages; science studies how the heavens go, religion how to go to heaven.[7]

Gould designates this principle by the acronym NOMA: 'non-overlapping magisteria'. Dawkins furiously repudiates it. He calls Gould, and all other natural scientists who likewise acknowledge NOMA, 'supine'. They are, he argues, no better than appeasers of unreason. While, as for theologians who profess to adhere to NOMA: theirs, he suggests, is simply an act of desperation, by people who see that otherwise their game is up. They're 'defining themselves into an epistemological Safe Zone'.[8] Here we have a sheer retreat from reason.

As someone who understands Christian faith in NOMA terms, I have to say that it doesn't exactly feel like a Safe Zone to me.

Again, consider Prince Andrei in *War and Peace*. What makes him such an interesting character is the way he's so consistently, and so seriously, exposed to the Question – both before and after his experience of epiphany on the battlefield of Austerlitz.

That epiphany is neither the beginning nor the end of his struggle with the Question; and the physical courage he shows as a soldier is very much of a piece with the moral courage that we see sustaining him, throughout his life, in that inner struggle. Forever restless, like Tolstoy himself (and like such other Tolstoyan characters as Pierre Bezuhov, or Konstantin Levin in *Anna Karenina*) he's driven to explore one existential standpoint after another. Although not an especially sophisticated thinker, he's distinguished by an exceptional instinct for truth-as-openness. Here, if you like, is Tolstoy's novelistic portrayal of what Kierkegaard, as a religious philosopher, calls *Angst*. That's to say, the specific sort of 'anxiety', 'dread' or 'stress' through which the Question goes to work.

Writing under the pseudonym 'Johannes Climacus', but no doubt fully meaning what he says, Kierkegaard declares it to be his ambition 'to make difficulties everywhere'.[9] He means this in the sense that life is 'difficult' for people like Prince Andrei. And here, it seems to me, we have the basic test of good theology in general: that it should serve to accentuate the proper work of religious faith in making life more 'difficult'.

'How I envy you your faith,' I've sometimes heard people wistfully say. I think they've been misled by religious propaganda. The way I understand it, there's nothing enviable about faith. On the contrary, 'How I envy you *your lack of faith*,' the unregenerate part of me is tempted to reply. If I wasn't troubled by faith, perhaps I could simply go with the flow and live life easy, as a complacent beneficiary of the dominant world order.

Beyond the metaphysical obsession with finding 'correct' answers to ultimate questions about the constitution of reality, there are, one might say, two basic species of intellectual discipline, essentially aiming, instead, to help 'make difficulties everywhere'. In both cases the project is to set oneself in the middle of the widest possible range of different points of view: different people's ways of seeing things, arising out of all sorts of different life-experience. It's to conjure up these various opposing points of view in one's mind, laying oneself as open as possible to what might be said in favour of each. And then it's to try and mediate between them, exercising the most imaginative sympathy. But the basic difference between the two disciplines lies in the range and character of the challenges that they set up in this way.

Thus, the two are:

1 trans-metaphysical philosophy – by which I mean a form of thinking the whole point of which is systematically to assemble the most open-to-all interplay between sophisticated philosophic viewpoints;
2 trans-metaphysical religious thought – by which I mean a form of thinking the whole point of which is to promote the most open-to-all debate, *also*, between intellectuals and non-intellectuals.

Both are projects for radicalizing the Question, by setting it into the context of the most open-to-all conversation. For, again, if one's never compelled to engage with the worldviews of people different from oneself, one's unlikely ever to be shaken free from the natural prejudices of one's own type. But *trans-metaphysical religious thought* makes good on what's surely the unique selling point of religion, in general, with regard to truth-as-openness. Namely: *its special ability, through the use of imagery and ritual, to draw both intellectuals and non-intellectuals together into a single community of conversation, about matters of the very deepest spiritual concern.*

Religious metaphysics is, indeed, the creation of a spiritual Safe Zone. It's an enterprise protecting the devout from the critical challenge of trans-metaphysical philosophy. Failing to see the proper nature of faith as a medium for truth-as-openness, it's preoccupied, instead, with seeking to defend the supposedly definitive truth-as-correctness of a certain religious orthodoxy. So it merely distracts attention from the true, existential substance of faith.

However, militant anti-religious scientism, or atheist metaphysics, of the kind so energetically popularized by Dawkins, is *likewise* the creation of a spiritual Safe Zone – in this case, protecting its adherents from the challenge of trans-metaphysical religious thought. Whatever its good intentions may be, the unfortunate effect of such thinking is to create a Safe Zone for intellectual snobbery.

The basic demand of truth-as-openness is that we step out of *both* these two Safe Zones, so as to enter into what the philosopher Gillian Rose has called the 'broken middle'.[10]

To occupy the 'broken middle' is to be more or less torn apart by pulls from every side, namely, pulls upon one's sympathy from all sorts of different voices, expressing different points of view and highlighting different, often even apparently incompatible aspects of reality. It's where one learns the wisdom of the true mediator, at full stretch – mediating between people of different cultures, different classes, different ages, different tastes and temperaments, different histories, different ambitions. And it therefore involves, not least, a truly patient mediation between the claims of religious tradition and those of secular rationalism.

The 'broken middle' is simply where the Question intrudes at its most direct and fiercest. What's 'broken' here are my defences against the Question, as the shaking power of the Question is mediated by my encounter with the otherness of all manner of other people, and their criticism of people like me, calling all my prejudices into doubt. For such wisdom to flourish requires, crucially, that one gives up one's natural craving for a sense of innocence. How, though, does one acquire the necessary inner strength to do so? The Christian theological answer is that it's only possible by God's grace. In fact, to my mind, this is just what 'God's grace' *means*. It's nothing other than that gift of inner strength.

Far from being a commitment to metaphysical 'belief without evidence', true Christian faith, as I understand it, is essentially a matter of trusting in God's grace to sustain one in the 'broken middle'. And the evidence for its truth is in the experience of being so sustained.

Colluding with bigots?

Although I believe in God – I'm a priest – I *don't* 'believe in belief'. The phrase 'belief in belief' is the (rather useful) coinage of Daniel Dennett. Much of his book *Breaking the Spell* is a polemic against 'belief in belief'.

By 'belief in belief' Dennett means the belief that there's something intrinsically good about belief in 'God', regardless of whether or not such belief is in fact true. 'Belief in belief' thus reinforces actual belief in 'God', but may also inspire continuing religious behaviour even where actual belief in 'God' is weak. And what especially concerns Dennett is the way in which residual 'belief in belief' so often inhibits even those who are quite clear about their own personal lack of belief in 'God' from criticizing religion in ways that might trouble believers.

'Believers in belief' value belief in 'God' for its morale-building effects. But, more importantly, 'belief in belief' represents a fundamental *disbelief* in controversy, where people are liable to find themselves challenged in their most sacred convictions. I entirely agree with Dennett that true respect for other people is by no means to be confused with a mere shrinking back from awkward controversy. On the contrary, it depends upon an absolutely intransigent respect for the claims of truth – I'm talking here about truth-as-openness. One isn't being truly respectful of other people just by failing to challenge their closed-mindedness.

I don't believe in religious belief, *simply as such*. Rather, I believe in whatever helps open us up to the moral challenge inherent in the suffering of other people, the wisdom of other people, or the sheer otherness of other people's world-view.

Therefore, I believe in the Question, as this helps open us up to those challenges by dissolving the resistance of un-questioned prejudice. I believe in whatever may intensify the prejudice-dissolving power of the Question; and I believe in God, *inasmuch as God is recognized as the Questioner.*

Belief in 'God' grounded in 'belief in belief' clearly *isn't* belief in God-as-Questioner. Rather, it's belief in the 'God' of controversy-suppressing *respectability-religion*. And when it comes to respectability-religion, I must say, I'm a follower of Jesus of Nazareth, as the Gospel of Matthew portrays him, declaring, 'Do not think I have come to bring peace to the earth; I have not come to bring peace, but a sword' (10.34). True religion isn't just about 'peace' in the sense of maintaining tight social order and control, either in society at large or within the little world of a sect. On the contrary, authentic faith in God – inasmuch as it represents an intransigent open-mindedness – will inevitably tend to stir conflict within the worshipping community.

Dennett for his part pays no heed to the possibility of belief in God unequivocally cut loose from 'belief in belief'. 'We can be quite sure', he remarks in passing, 'that . . . just about everybody who believes in God also believes in belief in God.'[11] But then, if I were to object to this rather airy statement, his rejoinder is obvious. How can I be truly serious in my repudiation of mere 'belief in belief' when, as a priest, I'm committed to *colluding* with so much religious belief that's crassly superstitious or bigoted?

It's the same with Dawkins, when he dismisses the articulate protagonists of 'understated, decent, revisionist religion' as 'numerically negligible'.[12] Of course, he isn't saying that small minorities in general, just because they're minorities, are never worth heeding. But to him it seems self-evident that this particular minority is straightaway discredited by what it *colludes* with.

And so, is it fair to say that people like me are merely in collusion with religious bigots? What, indeed, would it take for us not to be colluding with them? Is every offer of real conversation, made to people whose views one completely rejects, automatically a form of collusion with them? We believe in truth-as-openness. Truth-as-openness means openness towards all; we don't believe in excommunication. The trouble with rationalist sects, as such, is that they tend to replace real conversation with propaganda. And I'm, if anything, even more troubled by propaganda thinking – that is, any sort of thinking readily compatible with being expressed in propagandist form – than I am by superstition.

No, the primordial intellectual error of the religious bigots is that they've – in an especially fanatical way – confused religious faith with a form of metaphysical belief. And it seems to me, the non-bigoted people who are really colluding with them are none other than the 'scientific' rationalists who, likewise, make that confusion. People like Dawkins and Dennett are the ones who are really colluding with the bigotry of religious bigots, by getting caught up into a polemic in which the proper claims of truth-as-openness are equally ignored on both sides. They're colluding in a shouting match. I don't 'believe in belief', but I don't believe in shouting matches either. I believe in conversation framed, ideally, by contemplative prayer.

Openness versus control

However, I'm also very well aware that the problem's actually a bit more complicated than that.

Because it's true, it isn't only the religious bigots, and the militant atheists, who've confused faith with a form of metaphysical dogma.

In fact, I want to argue that this is really *the* fundamental confusion, still needing to be resolved, right at the very heart of the whole Christian theological tradition. Thus, on the one hand, there's faith properly understood as an intensified appetite for truth-as-openness, essentially expressed as a poetic accentuation of the Question, with God as Questioner. Here God's grace is experienced as the gift of inner strength enabling one to endure the stresses of the 'broken middle'. But then, on the other hand, there's what happens to the externals of faith, its imagery and rituals, to the extent that these have, on the contrary, become disconnected from the appetite for truth-as-openness. In which case, we find theology preoccupied with claims to exclusive metaphysical truth-as-correctness instead. And these claims tend to get caught up into projects of political control; they become the ideological basis for all sorts of manipulative threats and promises. The 'brokenness' of the 'broken middle' is a condition of *not* being in control. Metaphysical religion springs from an inability to endure this. So it closes down conversation precisely at the point where the 'middle' starts to break.

I don't 'believe in belief': I don't think that belief in 'God' *automatically* brings one closer to God. *Very often* it has the exact opposite effect. There are perhaps a good many believers in 'God', whose belief is on the surface identical with that of the very wisest true believers, yet who, deeper down, would actually be less distanced from the *real* truth of God were they to lose their belief altogether – if this lapse into unbelief derived from a resurgent appetite for truth-as-openness, and disgust at the closed-minded nature of the given Church culture around them, to which they'd hitherto been loyal. To be sure, I don't believe in unbelief either. Believing in unbelief would surely be just as crude an attitude as believing in belief. And besides, in the end, the option for simple unbelief is always an option for the basic untruth of imaginative impoverishment.

Still, that's a secondary matter. What's far more important, theologically, is the need for open-mindedness.

Thus, for example:

1 *The concept of God's 'almighty power'*
   Faith's experience of God-as-Questioner is an experience of
   life made meaningful by the divine Questioning, and what
   follows from that Questioning, as it never could have been
   in any other way. One may observe God-as-Questioner,
   also, 'anonymously' at work in non-theistic cultures. But,
   in the experience of the faithful, there's no other agency
   with anything like the power to make life meaningful that
   God, encountered as Questioner, has. To one who's truly been
   opened up by the Question, it's clear that none of the major
   rivals to God's Questioning has the same sort of power at
   all. No sort of opinionated bigotry has it; no mere passive
   acquiescence in the ways of the human herd; no propaganda
   ideology; no spirit of snobbery. None of these can render my
   life truly meaningful, the way that God, supra-metaphysically
   understood, can. When I address my prayers to 'almighty God',
   this is the unique power that I'm affirming.

   And, moreover, the ideal of perfect truth-as-openness
   demands a fundamental overcoming of resentment, self-
   pity and envy. For how can I be truly open towards other
   people when my moral outlook remains governed by such
   impulses? Therefore good theology – 'making difficulties
   everywhere' – systematically confronts us with the Problem
   of Evil. It insists that we accept whatever misfortunes may
   befall us without repining, with gratitude indeed, as gifts
   from God's creative love. All our misfortunes are to be
   accepted as gifts from the Questioner, loosening the bonds
   of complacent habit, and prompting us, ever more deeply,
   to question ourselves. But how can we, in actual practice,
   take them that way, when it means battling with the altogether more natural impulse merely to lash out instead? When
   we acknowledge God-as-Questioner, also, as Creator, we're
   being confronted with that elementary practical problem. The

more acutely we're confronted by it, the better, for only so can we be opened up as we need to be. At this level, good theology must, therefore, forever be intent on *accentuating* the Problem of Evil. How can faith in God as Creator be reconciled with our actual experience of evil in creation – if faith means renouncing bitterness? Everything depends upon that problem being rendered quite inescapable.

When, however, the appetite for truth-as-openness begins to lapse, and faith becomes an expression of something else, one of the prime indicators of the lapse – the miner's canary, so to speak – is what happens to the concept of God's 'almighty power'. Metaphysically, the way God is described in dogmatic terms, nothing appears to change – the poison gas is invisible. But that's just why we need to break free from metaphysics: so as to be alerted to the *underlying* change here.

The 'God' denounced in atheist polemic, such as that of Dawkins and Dennett, is a monstrous magic potentate, a Divine Despot, capable of anything, quite arbitrarily. The power of this imaginary figure no longer has anything whatever to do with truth-as-openness. Yet, of course, it isn't the atheists who've invented him. Manipulative religion naturally loves to invoke his supposedly 'infinite' magic power, the better to back up its threats and promises. And then, as a result, we're confronted with the Problem of Evil *in quite a different form*. It's no longer a problem that theology properly needs to accentuate. On the contrary, it's mutated into a set of rather obvious contradictions, absolutely serving to highlight what's gone wrong in such religion: its intrinsic cruelty and injustice. How can faith in God as Creator be reconciled with our actual experience of evil in creation – if God has *such* power? It's clear that 'God' the Divine Despot is neither loving nor just. The miracle stories in the New Testament may be read as enacted metaphors for the transformative irruption of truth-as-openness. But where faith no longer signifies any such irruption, what then? Every miraculous intervention of this 'God' becomes an act of capricious favouritism, for if so-and-so can be healed, or blessed, then why not such-and-such other people also? No amount of theological spin doctoring, however ingenious it may be in its mimicking of true theology, can disguise the absurdity here. In this degenerate form, the Problem of Evil does indeed become an overwhelming logical argument against false religion.

2 *The 'real presence' of God in the Eucharist*

Again, the unique selling point of true religion generally, it seems to me, is its capacity to enact truth-as-openness in the relationship between intellectuals and non-intellectuals. Its great virtue is the way it, at any rate, makes possible an ideal conversation-community, of maximum exposure to the Question, in which both categories of people are equally able to participate.

Every Christian Eucharist is a dramatic evocation of this ideal. And the 'higher' the sacramental understanding of the Eucharist, the clearer the evocation actually is. Thus, the work of the Eucharist may be regarded as twofold. On one level, it establishes a set of imaginative co-ordinates for conversation inspired by the Question: telling a sacred story, investing it with beauty, prayerfully setting the lives of those present into the context of that story's continuing flow. Here we have the Eucharist's work of *representation*. But on another level it also involves a work of *rendering-present*: the Eucharist not only works with secondary *re*-presentations of the Questioner, it also renders the Questioner sacramentally present.

In the Eucharist, the Questioner is rendered sacramentally present through the simple act of eating bread and drinking wine. Why is it done through eating and drinking? Basically, the answer is, because eating and drinking *aren't in any way intellectual acts*. The appreciation of a symbol as such is an intellectual act. Symbols may speak to everyone – that's their beauty – but when it comes to analysing and interpreting their meaning some people are better at it than others. For want of a better word, let's call these more skilled people 'intellectuals'. In dealing with any sort of representation intellectuals have a certain advantage. But the sacrament of the Eucharist renders God present in a way that's meant to point beyond that advantage. Granted, the sacrament of the Eucharist provides a rich context for symbolism. Yet, at the same time, by virtue of its sheer simplicity as a sacramental act, in a sense it also symbolically transcends all symbolism.

The simple acts of eating the consecrated 'body of Christ' and drinking the consecrated 'blood of Christ' are a more-than-just-symbolic enactment of the principle that God is equally present to both intellectuals and non-intellectuals. God's 'being present' to me means my having the God-given right to demand that my life-experience (as an implicit encounter with divine reality) be taken seriously by others and, ideally, through the celebration of the Eucharist, God-as-Questioner is opening up a space for conversation between intellectuals and non-intellectuals in which the actual life-experience of *all* will be accorded maximum respect. In the order of fallen nature, intellectuals are of course much better than non-intellectuals at securing respect for their life-experience. Their superior grasp of the arts of persuasion brings with it a temptation either to ignore, or else to misrepresent, the life-experience of others who are less well educated, and therefore less privileged. However, in the order of grace this temptation is overcome. The Eucharist, by its very nature, is essentially an anticipatory evocation of that overcoming. At the Lord's Table, God is just as *present* to the brain-damaged individual who has no language at all as to the most sophisticated theological interpreter of the occasion. The point is that both are equal in the simple acts of eating and drinking.

21

How is God present in these acts? Thomas Aquinas, seeking to express the more-than-just-symbolic nature of this presence, famously came up with the formula that the bread and wine have been 'transubstantiated'. They haven't only been transformed into a symbolic reminder of historic events, attached to theological theory, for intellectuals to enjoy and play around with. No, they've been transformed at quite another level. Adopting the Aristotelian philosophic distinction between 'substance' and 'accident', Aquinas suggests that, whereas symbolism works with the 'accidental' surface of phenomena, the eucharistic bread and wine are transformed in their very inmost 'substance'.

For my part, I can't conceive of any better dogmatic formulation.

But Aquinas's 'high' understanding of the sacrament only makes sense so long as it's quite clearly incorporated into a theological project for the advancement of truth-as-openness. As soon as the appetite for truth-as-openness begins to lapse, and other motives start to take over, the dogmatic notion of transubstantiation loses its meaning. Then it becomes exactly what Dawkins and Dennett consider it to be, namely, perhaps the most ridiculous instance of pure mumbo-jumbo in the whole Christian theological tradition. *They* certainly don't see it as having anything to do with an affirmation of human rights, or a challenge to the all-too-natural corporate conceit of the well educated, as a privileged class! On the contrary, all that they see here is a bit of non-sense, the main purpose of which is to feed the corporate conceit of the Roman Catholic clergy: flattering them, as the regular performers of such a wondrous bit of magic. And, of course, the Protestant Reformers already saw it the same way. Number 28 of the Thirty-Nine Articles that are meant to set out the doctrinal foundation of the Church of England expressly denounces all talk of 'transubstantiation' as being, in essence, 'superstitious'.

I think that the authors of this Article were, in fact, completely mistaken with regard to the original essence of the doctrine, as Aquinas intended it. But yes, it *is* ambiguous. It's ambiguous in the way that every dogmatic formula for faith, purely and simply as such, always is: everything depends on how it's *lived*.

3 *The politics of Easter*

At the same time, the infinitude of the infinite Question makes people restless, often to the extent of rendering them, from the point of view of the world's rulers, subversive. It's forever dissolving moral prejudice, but rulers tend to have a big investment in moral prejudice, as a key element in the ideology that's supposed to give legitimacy to their rule. In any case, those who are dedicated to the ideal of perfect truth-as-openness are unlikely to be unstinting admirers of politicians dedicated to ideologies of control. And right at the heart of Christian faith is a story symbolically dramatizing this entire species of conflict; the whole proper thrust of which is to energize resistance to conversation-closing oppression.

Faith is what 'saves' us. But what exactly do we mean by 'salvation'? In principle, the Easter story defines it. Here, God raises to life a crucified dead dissident. It's a sort of *judo throw*: using the impetus of the opponent, toppled off balance, to throw them. God uses the tremendous poetic energy inherent in the Roman judicial practice of crucifixion, so as, in the most poetic way, to overthrow the whole value-system that this judicial practice is meant to reinforce.

For crucifixion is the most vicious contradiction, a barbaric act envisaged by its perpetrators as a necessary measure for the defence of civilization. The pagan Romans took those they saw as political threats to the good order of civilization, and put them to death in the most public, most theatrical, most cruel, most lingering and so most terrifying way. It was a beautifully calculated act of terrorist propaganda.

Nor was there anyone, in that world, who protested that this was an offence against civilized values. On the contrary, it was regarded as a regrettable necessity, without which civilization would be mortally endangered. According to the prevailing viewpoint in pagan Rome, civilization was, first and foremost, an achievement of controlling power: the more spectacular, the better. The law and order that the pagan Romans achieved allowed all sorts of civilized conversation to flourish, incidentally. But they didn't identify the *essence* of civilization with the allure of good open conversation, informed by the Question. They never acknowledged the proper sovereignty of that ideal. And nothing made this non-acknowledgement clearer, poetically, than the showy ruthlessness of crucifixion. Its whole purpose, after all, was to obviate the need for truly open conversation between rulers and ruled.

Every alternative, as a basis for civilization, to the ideal of perfect truth-as-openness is, one might say, an ideology of control. True Christian faith amplifies the appetite for truth-as-openness. And so it recognizes the crucifixion of Jesus as symbolizing the destructive nature of *all* such ideologies. For Jesus, here, surely represents the ideal of perfect truth-as-openness, an ideal openness towards all – even outcasts, even one's enemies – uplifted above all other ideals. The raising up of this crucified dissident, from death, thus becomes the definitive representation of the true civilization-founding will of God-as-Questioner. What God-as-Questioner demands is perfect truth-as-openness; the action of those who brought about Jesus' crucifixion becomes a symbol of 'civilized' contempt for that ideal in general. Whenever the Romans crucified anyone, they were making a powerful symbolic statement, to the effect that might is right. But when the first Christians affirmed that God had raised to life this one who'd been crucified, and that this event defined 'salvation' for all of us,

24

it threw that older Roman symbolism right up into the air and down.

How, exactly, did God bring them to this moment of insight? I don't know, and am content not to know. I just want to urge that we shouldn't be distracted by questions about the mechanism. Only one thing matters, namely, that we should be clear about the original logic of the resultant symbolism. Jesus is our Saviour by virtue of his being first crucified, and then seen to be raised. That he was first *crucified* is, precisely, crucial. If he hadn't been, if he'd died in any other way, then I don't think he could have been our Saviour. Any interpretation of the Easter story that fails to engage with the original judo-throw reversal here of the old pagan-Roman symbolism of the cross empties it of its properly saving truth.

But, in actual fact, that's exactly what does happen, as soon as the appetite for truth-as-openness ceases to be the chief motivation of Christian theology. Then, the original politics is washed out of the story. It becomes quite unimportant *how* Jesus died. No longer properly perceived as the symbolic embodiment of truth-as-openness – insisting on the Question and directly confronting all rival idolatries of control – he becomes instead a merely totemic figure.

True faith, when it affirms that the Church is called to be the 'body of Christ', begins from the understanding that the crucified but risen Christ represents the indwelling of God within each one of us. That is, within the innate potential for truth-as-openness of every individual soul. But Christ as a totemic figure is, on the contrary, a mere symbolic *projection* of the Church community as a project of control. No longer the symbolic representative of all authentic human individuality, waiting to be unlocked by the Question, his uniqueness as an individual now, on the contrary, merely serves to ground the unique authority claimed by the controllers of the Church.

Then, as the original historic significance of crucifixion is forgotten, the dominant theological understanding of Christ's saving work tends to become increasingly mythic. The Easter story is put on the same level as the story of Adam and Eve, which it reverses. It becomes a mythic tale of substitutionary atonement: the story of a divine superhero, who dies (it doesn't really matter how, the historic judo-throw logic is lost) to remove the burden of humanity's guilt, on condition that we then honour him with an impassioned loyalty to 'his' Church. (Indeed, unconditional divine love becomes thoroughly conditional, in this sense!) And so theology degenerates, to become what the atheists think it always is. In place of a poetic amplification of the Question, all that we're left with is the mere ideology of a self-serving institution.

An argument for hope

In what follows, I want to develop an argument for hope. For it actually seems to me that we're in a better position nowadays to clarify the fundamental difference between true Christian faith, *in itself*, and its attendant metaphysical dogma, than ever before.

As I've said, this isn't just intended to be an apologetic argument, defending faith against its atheistic critics. The stimulus of atheistic polemic may well be one of the factors that help prod us towards this clarification, and so I've begun from that prod. But what really interests me far more than any apologetic argument is the simple question:

> What would it mean for a true seriousness about truth-as-openness to become, in vital reality, the one and only prime determinant of Christian corporate practice?

For that's the ideal understanding of the 'kingdom of God' which I now see potentially opening up before us.

Thus, I want to try and consider this new opening-up

- in relation to changing secular contexts (Chapter 2);
- in relation to the authority of Scripture and tradition (Chapter 3);
- in relation to the Church's rites of initiation (Chapter 4);
- in relation to our structures of Church leadership and unity (Chapter 5).

Since I'm a priest of the Church of England, the result is a 'reimagining of Anglicanism'. It's an argument for hope, in the first instance, addressed to the Church of England; then, to the larger Anglican world that has grown from it, and remains most directly exposed to its influence. Notwithstanding all the various troubles by which we're from time to time afflicted, paradoxically perhaps, I think that this is in principle a very good time to be an Anglican, and more particularly a member of the Church of England. I'll try and say why.

However, I'm not only writing for other Anglicans. The underlying hope in question is clearly one that I hope Christians of every tradition will also come to share.

2

'Beyond good and evil'

'Crucial'

Let's think, now, about adjectives.

This 'Question', which theology is charged not to answer but to intensify: the infinite, the forever shape-shifting, the all too obvious, the elementary, the simple, the naively ever-recurrent, the sobering, the anxiety generating, the potentially terrible, the all-endangering, the constantly suppressed, the elusive, the mystical, the shaking, the God's-grace Question. So far I've simply written it with a capital Q. How, though, shall we also identify it *audibly*? For that, we surely need to choose one particular adjective.

I'm talking about *the* Question, the question of questions: for all of us, in principle, the big, the burning, the vital, the *crucial* Question.

No term's perfect for the particular technical purpose I have in mind. But my choice, in what follows, is for '*crucial*'. It derives from the Latin word *crux*, meaning 'cross'; I've chosen it for the way it evokes the memory of the crucified. What I'm looking for here is the best form of Church life for transmitting the 'crucial' Question: that is, the decisive one, for the welfare of each individual soul.

The solidarity of the shaken

My chief objection to the atheism of thinkers like Dawkins and Dennett is that they've made it far too easy for themselves by, basically, just ignoring the proper criterion for religious truth. Namely: how well it imaginatively opens up and holds open the crucial Question.

Compare *Nietzsche*. I think that Nietzsche is an altogether more formidable critic, inasmuch as he doesn't oppose Christianity on the basis of atheism, as a metaphysical dogma. (Unlike Dawkins and Dennett, Nietzsche isn't so much an atheist as the philosophical devotee of another god: 'Dionysus'.) But, instead, he focuses his critique precisely on the Christian tradition's repeated betrayals of God-as-Questioner.

Nevertheless, at another level, Nietzsche, likewise, also makes things all too easy for himself. Thus, his basic aim is summed up in the title of his book *Beyond Good and Evil*. By 'good and evil', here, he means the conventional moral categories of what he calls 'herd morality': in effect, any code of ethics untroubled by the crucial Question. Nietzsche sets out to develop an ethos, a moral discipline of the imagination, that will, far more decisively he thinks than any form of Christianity, point 'beyond good and evil', towards that source of trouble. His stories of 'Zarathustra' are designed to do this; while in his other writings he prepares the ground for these with an extensive critique of actually existing Christian 'herd morality', and everything he sees as being, in any way, either complicit with or akin to it. The only trouble is that at the same time he also very greatly simplifies matters by a priori restricting what one might call his missionary outreach. He has no interest in the dissemination of wisdom, other than within the confines of the most exclusive intellectual elite. And that allows him quite shamelessly – manipulatively indeed – to *flatter* his readers, they being the potential elite in question. Moreover, he spares himself the difficulty of having to think seriously about questions of community organization, in the service of 'Dionysus'. Because the only community involved, for him, is the community already constituted by the sheer act of reading his books.

In short, it seems to me that Nietzsche has muddled together two quite different strategic principles that really need to be kept distinct. On the one hand, there's the ideal principle of solidarity binding together all those whose world-view has been significantly shaken by the workings of the crucial Question: a solidarity of mutual respect based, purely and simply, on that shared experience of having been shaken open, pitched towards truth-as-openness. Let's call this the 'solidarity of the shaken'.[1] And on the other hand, there's what one might call a 'solidarity among philosophers', which, by contrast, is a form of solidarity bound up with self-congratulatory attachment to shared educational privilege, creatively appropriated. Indeed, he's an advocate of philosopher-solidarity at its most extreme. He believes not only in an absolute openness to the crucial Question but also in the most ruthless, undisguised elitism; he fails to see that these are, at the deepest level, contradictory impulses.

Of course, philosophers are in some ways better able to *express* the experience of being shaken open by the crucial Question than non-philosophers are. But as soon as you make that expressive ability, rather than the actual experience of *shaken-openness in itself*, the basis for solidarity, then it seems to me that you are liable to lose touch with the proper truth-potential intrinsic to the Question as such. It starts to disappear behind the dictates of intellectual-elite ideology, deriving from the elite's corporate vanity. This is Plato's old error. Plato's version of intellectual-elite ideology, in addition, exalted philosophy over poetry. Nietzsche doesn't do that; his 'Dionysian' wisdom takes shape as a form of philosophy altogether infused with poetry, from the roots up. But the result is just that he represents a more lyrically flamboyant elitism.

I'm a Christian priest, basically, because I believe in the solidarity of the shaken, and because I can see no real alternative to popular religion when it comes to promoting that ideal, in all its true difference from solidarity among philosophers.

Yet, by the same token, equally I want to argue for a strict theoretical priority of the solidarity of the shaken over the confessional *solidarity of Christians with Christians as Christians*, even where the two are closest conjoined in practice. For it seems to me that what Jesus, in the New Testament, calls the 'kingdom of God', or the 'kingdom of heaven', is, in fact, none other than the solidarity of the shaken, as framed by Hebrew religious tradition. What else, after all, is this 'kingdom' if not a solidarity-principle? And what other qualifications are there for participation in it besides an experience of being shaken out of the ordinary complacent moral closures of everyday life? Jesus is speaking about the solidarity of the shaken in the theological thought-forms given him by his immediate cultural context. But, again, the logically foundational move that I want to make as a theologian is to focus on the lived substance of what's involved here rather than the theoretical form.

In other words: what in the end counts for salvation is surely the actual experience of being shaken open, and its being made a basis for solidarity, far more than any sort of 'correct' theological expression for that process. Christian faith is only valid insofar as it consistently outbids its critics' appeal to intellectual integrity, removing every last potential hiding-place for motives other than the pure love of truth-as-openness.

The proper ultimate goal of Christian mission is surely to try and help realise the kingdom of God. As I'd see it, this means to develop the most vivid possible approximation to the solidarity of the shaken. But then true Christian theology is all about distinguishing what underlies such solidarity, the pure love of truth-as-openness, from the demands of what one might call 'Church ideology', as this is driven, on the contrary, by the mere corporate vanity, and self-seeking will to power, of Christian communities and institutions. Church ideology hides behind opaque, superficial claims to theological correctness. However, I'm committed to theology essentially envisaged as an attempt to render the solidarity of Christians with Christians as *transparent* as possible to the solidarity of the shaken. Which is, of course, both a much narrower principle than the solidarity of Christians with Christians, since not all Christians are shaken open, and also a much broader one, inasmuch as it embraces all who are shaken open, whether Christian or not.

And I also want to develop an argument for hope: *never before have we Christian theologians been in such a good position as we are now for thinking through what such transparency involves.*

'One holy catholic and apostolic'

What sort of a Church is best equipped to promote the solidarity of the shaken? Consider the classic affirmation of the Nicene Creed: 'We believe in one holy catholic and apostolic Church'.

There are two pairs of terms here. To be 'one' and 'holy' are surely the ambitions of any religious community: the connotations of 'catholic' and 'apostolic' are, in the first instance, more specifically Christian. All sorts of things have over time come to be associated with the ideas of catholicism and apostolicity. But the Creed may perhaps recall us to what's fundamental. Catholicism is a particular form of unity. Apostolicity is a particular form of holiness. And I want to argue that, at the deepest level, these two ideals are actually best understood as the twin aspects of a true transparency to the solidarity of the shaken. Thus:

1 *Catholic unity*
   Of course, in common English usage 'Catholic' mostly just means either 'not Protestant' or, when applied to forms of Anglicanism, 'not only Protestant'. A key task of theology, however, is surely to try and rescue the vocabulary of Christian tradition where common usage has reduced it to the

mere demarcation of ecclesiastical faction-identities. So let's
go back to the origins of the word.

The earliest Christian writer to use the Greek term,
ekklesia katholikē, 'catholic Church', is Ignatius of Antioch,
in his *Epistle to the Smyrnaeans*, around the year 110:

> The sole Eucharist you should consider valid is one that
> is celebrated by the bishop himself, or by some person
> authorised by him. Where the bishop is to be seen, there let
> all his people be; just as wherever Jesus Christ is present,
> we have the catholic church.[2]

Here, the word 'catholic' has the given meaning of 'general',
'universal' or 'world-wide'. The immediate contrast is
with Gnostic guru-led groups, promoting a Docetic Chris-
tology, the view that Christ only 'appeared' to be, but was
not really, flesh and blood. Gnostic Docetism is, in essence,
a reflection of elitism: the Gnostics purported to worship the
true, 'spiritual' Christ, as opposed to the merely 'corporeal'
Christ of the bishop-led Church, full of less-well-educated
folk. Straightaway in this context 'catholic' therefore means
anti-elitist or broadly inclusive. In Ignatius' *Epistle to the
Philadelphians* we also see him engaged in a continuation of
St Paul's struggle against hard-line Jesus-Judaism. Gnostic
groups in effect excluded anyone lacking a certain level of
education; Jesus-Judaism was only open to those Gentiles
who were prepared to become observant Jews, for instance,
in matters of diet. Ignatius' notion of the true 'catholic'
Church was distinguished from both these two alternatives
by its much greater openness to all-comers. When he calls
his Church 'catholic' he's emphasizing its coherence, in
loyalty to its bishops; but the whole point of this 'catholic'
form of coherence was that it didn't depend upon exclusion,
in the way that rival forms did.

And thereafter this is the consistent pattern: that those who
seek to uphold the 'catholic' Church as such, in polemical

terms, are always vaunting the coherence of their community, in openness to people of every class and ethnicity. The Roman Catholic Church gets its name from its apologists pointing to its unique trans-national coherence, as contrasted especially to the schismatic nature of Protestantism, and the lack of any adequate principle of resistance, within Protestant Church culture, against further schismatic disintegration. Every schism is an act of exclusion; for that reason, it's a failure to be properly catholic.

But let's move on, then, just a little further, in the same direction. Looking beyond these particular polemical contexts, how might we formulate the ultimate ideal of true catholicism, as a general principle? I propose that we define it as

> an absolute maximum of unity, in the sense of open conversational engagement, embracing the widest possible range of both social groups and approaches to doctrine.

Note: this definition fits perfectly with the underlying imperatives of the solidarity of the shaken. For the more 'catholic' a community is, along these lines, the more space it gives for the sorts of encounter, with the otherwise minded, which generate the crucial Question. And, by the same token, the less licence it allows for dogmatic habits of mind, designed to protect people from the trouble of that challenge.

'Catholicism', so defined, is, first of all, the purest possible antithesis to any sort of schismatic thinking. To the true believer in this ideal, there can never be any legitimate reason for demonstratively walking out of one's old church, unexpelled – short, perhaps, of one's having been so crushed by bullying as to have one's very sanity endangered. Regardless of how corrupt the old church may be, or how fierce one's dissent from its prevailing ethos, no voluntary walkout could be regarded as a triumphal act; none could ever be justified merely in the name of ideological purity. (Not even where the supposed purity in question calls itself 'Catholic'!) But, at the same time – and for the self-same reason – true catholic unity, as I understand it, is also the sheer opposite to any form of coercive unity. Coercion in the Church context operates by hate-filled threats of exclusion, but the whole point of true catholicism is to be an organized witness to God's love for all. And, therefore, I'd argue, every coercive act of excommunication, or threat of excommunication, or any declaration of being in 'impaired communion', on the part of the majority, is, by its nature, a failure of catholicism, just as much as is the schismatic act of walking out, by a minority. No one who excommunicates, or threatens to excommunicate, others, or who declares themselves to be in 'impaired communion' with others, truly believes in the 'catholic Church', the way I'd understand that concept. Nor can anyone safely be allowed to minister in such a Church who indulges in coercive threats, either to secede or to excommunicate their opponents. Yet, besides that one strict prohibition, there'd be no room in a true catholic Church for any *further* discipline of censorship whatever. Such a Church would be one in which the wheat and the weeds were left to grow freely together, until harvest, lest in rooting out the latter one also root out the former by mistake (Matthew 13.24–30).

Once upon a time I quite seriously considered becoming a Roman Catholic. And if I already belonged to the Roman Catholic Church, I certainly wouldn't leave. The more I think about it, though, the clearer it appears to me that Roman Catholicism has never been anything like catholic enough. It's always been far too Roman, in other words, too imperialistically censorious, to be, in the ideal sense, catholic.

But then, it seems to me, no Church yet exists, that *is*.

One had better ask, rather, what sort of Church might, one day, *develop into* an authentically catholic one, and how? It would, in the first place, be a community that accorded great respect to theology, as a discipline of the most open and free spirited conversation. But, paradoxically, there might nevertheless be some advantages in its not having had any very strong theological tradition, hitherto. For at least that means there's no over-dominant orthodoxy already in place, liable to inhibit fresh theological creativity. Even though muddle is no virtue in itself, it may, in some ways, help for a Church to have developed something of a higgledy-piggledy accumulation of diverse intellectual styles. (As Anglicanism has.)

Also – notwithstanding that true catholicism, as I'd understand it, is essentially a mode of transparency to the solidarity of the shaken, which is very much a counter-cultural phenomenon – it may not be altogether a disadvantage for a Church to have emerged from a Constantinian past. (Again, as Anglicanism has.) In some ways it may be easier for an established Church to find space for the solidarity of the shaken than it would be for a counter-culturally sectarian one. At all events, a Church with a history of being unified by shared privilege rather than by shared doctrine inherits fewer positive *theological* barriers to the solidarity of the shaken. The devotional life of such a Church is liable to be highly pluralistic. Insofar as it continues to hanker after privilege, this hankering will of course always remain an obstacle. But if its privileges then gradually melt away, the pluralistic Church culture that remains, as the side effect of that history of privilege, may become quite a favourable environment for the development of authentic catholicity. Just so long, that's to say, as the opportunity is recognized for what it is.

Furthermore, it clearly does help to belong to a global communion (like that of Anglicanism). The Holy Spirit is cunning, always ready to be creative with the side effects of ugly history; and this is not least the case when it comes to the long-term consequences of imperialism. The gospel originated as an outcry of protest against the savagery of the Roman Empire. However, it was the law and order of that Empire, and the communications network it enabled, which made it possible for the early Church to spread so fast and so far. Other subsequent empires have likewise contributed to the creation, at last, of a truly global Church. All that now remains is for the new global Church to learn, as never before, genuinely non-coercive forms of conversational discipline, with no one excluded. (But I'll come back to this in Chapter 5.)

Antique institutional churches, like the Church of England, are often such frustrating organizations to belong to, and sometimes downright embarrassing. Wouldn't it be better to try and find some cleaner, more fluid, affinity group religiousness, not involving so much compromise? No, that would be too easy! I believe in the 'catholic' Church. And this means staying in communities of conversation even with people many of whose attitudes I utterly deplore; close bonded together with them, for better or worse, very much as a family, not as a club. For the true wisdom of faith doesn't lie in disengaged innocence. But, on the contrary, it's *all about* learning how to negotiate the 'broken middle'.

2 *Apostolic holiness*

Very similar problems arise, again, in the case of 'apostolicity': here too various church-factional notions immediately need to be discounted.

For instance, in the context of debates over the ordination of women to the priesthood and episcopate, some people have pointed to the maleness of the 12 Apostles, to argue that an 'apostolic' Church, as such, can only have male clergy. I have to say that this strikes me as an almost blasphemous trivializing of the concept, with no rationale to it, at all, other than a form of church-factionalism.

In Pentecostal theology, on the contrary, 'apostolicity' tends to be associated with the sheer enthusiasm of the very early Church, manifested above all in the gift of speaking in tongues. Unlike the association with male priesthood, the association with speaking in tongues does at least relate to the counter-cultural distinctiveness of New Testament Christianity, in its original context. But speaking in tongues, awe-inspiring though it may be, is surely more a gift of God's mercy for the relief of mental stress, among the down-trodden, than a practice *necessarily* consequent upon one's being shaken open, in prayer, by the Questioning of God-as-Questioner.

Other traditions, meanwhile, link 'apostolicity', in the first instance, to the notion of the Apostolic Succession, the unbroken chain of authority conferred by the laying-on of hands, from the first Apostles onwards. That, though, is surely more a symbolic pointer towards the demands of apostolicity than any sort of guarantee that they're fulfilled. And so what are the demands that it points towards? It's clear that for St Paul what made one an 'apostle' was that one had *seen* the risen Christ (1 Corinthians 9.1, 15.3–9). The apostles, in other words, were the first witnesses to the good news of God's great judo throw at Easter. One possible definition, then, might be that apostolicity is just

> whatever follows from a fresh connection back to the sheer shaking-open power of that event.

The violence of crucifixion symbolically represents every sort of bid to suppress the public asking of the crucial Question; the resurrection of the crucified is a great symbolic counter-vindication of all that's thereby been suppressed; and an apostolic community is, very simply, one in which the symbolism still functions that way, as opposed to having been reduced to a mere totem of Church-ideological identity.

But there are two basic aspects to this. When *John Keble*, for example, in his momentous Assize Sermon of 1833, called for a renewed 'apostolic' spirit in the Church of England, he was appealing to one aspect. Keble's great ally, Newman, in retrospect, saw this sermon – later published under the title *National Apostasy* – as the launch of the Oxford Movement. The immediate occasion for Keble's argument was a parliamentary decision to reduce the number of bishoprics in Ireland. However, the manner in which that decision had been made seemed to him symptomatic of a pervasive lack of proper respect for the Anglican ecclesiastical establishment. It was clear that the Church lacked adequate moral authority. This was in part because all too many of the clergy were absentees: gentlemen appointed to their posts by virtue of their family's status, and altogether more interested in following the typical pursuits of the gentry than in being proper pastors to their people. As Newman put it:

> At present [the Church of England] is too much a Church for the Aristocracy, and the poor *through* the Aristocracy.[3]

It was the Church of the landed ruling class and their allies, plus whoever else was willing to be deferential to them. Those who weren't prepared to be deferential had largely left, to become Nonconformists; Keble's advocacy of, as he put it, a true, 'apostolic' Anglicanism was a critical response to this situation. Thus, he associated apostolicity, very much, with a willing acceptance of poverty, by the Church's ministers, for the gospel's sake. Apostolicity, as the Oxford Movement understood it, was essentially a campaigning critique of secular ruling-class complacency within the Church.

Surely, though, true apostolicity is the antithesis to *any* sort of corporate complacency. And therefore it stands opposed not only to the contamination of Church life by secular ruling-class complacency of the sort that so troubled Keble,

Newman and their followers but also, and just as much, to more ostensibly devout forms of self-seeking.

Indeed, consider how the apostles themselves are portrayed in Mark, and in those parts of Matthew and Luke that appear to be drawn from the Marcan tradition: it's anything but a flattering picture. Most notably, Jesus rebukes them for their shameless squabbling over the question of their comparative status within the nascent Church, their competitive boasting about their closeness to him (Mark 9.33–37, 10.35–37, 41–45, and parallels). What does it mean to affirm one's belief in an 'apostolic' Church? From the Marcan point of view, perhaps the most important way in which the apostles remain a model for those who come after them is that they're the people who've most directly heard that rebuke. They've had that direct foretaste of the day of judgement; their souls have been seared by that paradigmatic experience of shame. Hence, they've become symbols of *corporate repentance.*

A Church that's authentically apostolic is one that relates in the truest possible way to its past. What sort of relationship to one's past is most hospitable to the crucial Question? Surely, everything here depends upon an honest *owning* of difficult historical memories. It's crucial that we should fully own our belonging to the Church, both as a communion of saints and as a communion of sinners. In fact, I think that a Church that was really serious about this would give a serious amount of liturgical time to the task. It would have a very different sort of *liturgical calendar* from any that yet exists. Currently, the Church's year is shaped, first, by a series of festivals celebrating its glorious foundation and, second, by a series of saints' days, to celebrate the glories of its tradition. A truly apostolic Church would no doubt continue to treasure all these memories. But, in my view, it would also do something else. Far more than any Church today, it would give dedicated time – a day here, a week there – to remembering its own historic record of corporate sin. An apostolic Church, filled with the risen power of the crucified Questioner, would above all be an honest Church – what, though are we to say of a Church that still fails to give serious liturgical time to remembering, and repenting, its persecution of the Jews? Or its violent intolerance of 'heretics' and other minorities, its collusion with slavery, its bloodthirsty encouragement of 'crusading' warfare, and all its innumerable other historic surrenders to the spirit that crucifies? Such a Church can scarcely be accounted altogether honest. The Church is called to be the 'body of Christ'. And our faith affirms that he 'bore' our corporate sins 'in his body' on the cross (1 Peter 2.24). What else, then, does it mean for the Church to be the 'body of Christ' if not that we too should truly 'bear' the corporate sins of our fore-runners as our own, in imitative response to his symbolic 'bearing' of ours?

Maybe it even helps, in this regard, to belong to a Church like the Church of England, so much of whose history appears, now that times have changed, so *patently* discred-itable! Once we were a Church whose whole identity was defined by privilege. Now that we've largely lost our old status of privilege we're a bit bewildered. We no longer quite know who we are. The Church of England, when it first split from Rome, was meant to occupy a privileged 'middle' place in English society, but now the middle, where we are, has been broken. Thank God – for there couldn't be a theologically more stimulating situation. It means that Anglicanism, which has hitherto had only the most mediocre of theological traditions, is now, for the first time, starting to simmer with creative thought.

But where's the Spirit leading us? I think that the Church of England's clear ecumenical calling is to become *a pioneeringly repentant ex-oppressor Church.*

The 'European exception': its providential aspect

Never before have Christian theologians been in such a good position to comprehend the proper nature of 'one holy catholic and apostolic' Church – throwing off mere Church ideology and opening towards perfect truth-as-openness – as we now are.

One reason for this is peculiarly European: because of the long-term and continuing decline in the political power and wealth of religious institutions, generally, in Europe, so unlike elsewhere in the world. I think that we need to understand this as, in essence, a necessary purgative experience and, hence, as a great gift of divine providence.

Of course, there's much about the process that's regrettable. In the first place, the weakening of so many European churches appears to be part of a broader trend, affecting more or less all forms of organization dependent on public-spirited volunteers. It can scarcely be regarded as a healthy development that the number of people willing to dedicate themselves to unpaid work for such organizations, in general, is diminishing. Second, from the Enlightenment onwards, the cause of secularization has been pushed forward by a series of intellectual fashions notable for their basic lack of serious conversational engagement with free-spirited theology. And, third, not only is the experience of decline demoralizing for the churches but also it often tempts them, by way of supposed remedy, to resort to the crudest, most manipulative sorts of propaganda evangelism, in effect surrendering to the prevalent ethos of consumerism, as a result.

Yet, the power that the churches once had, and have now lost, was so corrupting! We're charged to spread the gospel to all people, but it's no good if what we spread is only a simulacrum of the gospel: if it's more a form of pious ideology, dressed up in the mere externals of orthodox belief than real theology. The moral health of a church isn't to be measured by its simple ability to attract and keep members. After all, this is always easier to do if one cheapens the gospel. And, with that in view, let's actually thank God that the European churches have to such a large extent now lost the old, unnecessary protection that churches still enjoy elsewhere, of a pervasive, consensual 'belief in belief'. Several critics have remarked how very American the urgency of Dennett's attack on 'belief in belief' feels. This is just because that sort of second-order 'belief' remains so much stronger in the USA than in Europe.

In any society there will always be people who shy away from confronting religious irrationality, for fear of giving offence. But, over and above that, 'belief in belief' flourishes in the USA, above all, by virtue of the close connection, there, between most forms of religion and *patriotism*. As is indicated by all those smart flags, the Stars and Stripes, that one sees in American churches, flags which are so unattractive to many non-Americans. The lack of any one established church means that every church is equally able to identify itself with the patriotic, civil religious cause. And in such an ethnically plur- alistic culture, of course, patriotism appears all the more necessary, as a unifying factor. To the extent that religious belief is seen as helping promote patriotism, it becomes patriotic to 'believe in belief'. To be too overtly critical of one's fellow citizens' religion seems to be unpatriotically divisive: so it is that a professed unbeliever can scarcely hope to make much of a political career in the USA. There are of course also some parts of Europe where patriotic sentiment is closely intertwined with religious faith. Poland is the obvious example – which is why Poland is the most religiously observant society in Europe.[4] But elsewhere the churches have, for good reason, tended to become more wary of patriotism. The trauma of the First World War largely discredited one species of devout patriotism. And then the co-opting of patriotic sentiment, in another form, by the Nazis and Fascists reinforced that lesson, as did the violent experience of Northern Ireland and the Balkans.

However strong certain forms of truculent patriotism still are in the member states of the European Union, for the most part it no longer has anything like the same pseudo-religious fervent uplift that inspired the combatants in the First World War, or the Nazis and Fascists after that. And therefore, on the whole, it no longer provides the sort of moral energy that churches can parasitically thrive on, as some of them used to. This means that the churches can't depend upon patriotic 'belief in belief' to shelter them from critique.

Here's an emergent culture in which churches can no longer expect to enjoy moral authority as a matter of course. In such a culture moral authority really does have to be *earned*. To an increasing extent, a church can only gain it by being seen to cultivate the most transparent Honesty: a true openness to criticism. But isn't this, then, the very sort of environment in which genuine religious truth is most likely to flourish? 'Many that are first will be last, and the last first': the Church of England in particular quite clearly belongs to the former category. And no doubt we have a good deal more humiliation ahead of us, in worldly terms. Thank God, though, for this is a form of pruning. It's preparing us, as a Church, the only way we ever could be prepared, for the possibility, at least, of truly momentous fresh insight. We have to die a bit in order to live.

Third modernity

Furthermore, another all-transforming new development is that Christian theology now has to respond, as never before, to the pressures coming from single-issue *public conscience movements*, of every kind. By which I mean campaigning movements, independent of any particular religious or party-political organization, whose goal is simply to make a difference by appealing to and cultivating the public conscience.

The first historical example of such a movement was the campaign for the abolition of slavery, which, as an organized enterprise, dates back, in Britain, to 1787. But there's been a great proliferation of them more recently, with a surge from the 1960s onwards: campaigns for human rights, peace campaigns, anti-racist campaigns, feminist campaigns, campaigns for global economic justice, green campaigns and so forth.

These, in general, actually seem to me to be the nearest sort of thing there is to a *direct* organizational expression of the solidarity of the shaken.

In my book *God and Modernity* I tried to sketch out a grand narrative account of the emergence of the possibility of the solidarity of the shaken, explicitly invoked as the guiding principle of actual organizations.[5] Why a grand narrative? Partly, this is just a matter of scale: as the solidarity of the shaken is a cosmopolitan ideal, it requires a narrative, setting out where it's come from and what it aspires to, framed in cosmopolitan terms. And partly it's because I want to affirm the solidarity of the shaken as a principle of the most vivid political hope. Thus, a grand narrative is simply an attempt to justify such hope, as feeding into a cosmopolitan evangelistic enterprise. It's a big story of progress, in that sense. One hears a great deal of fuzzy talk these days about our living in a 'postmodern age'. But the most cogent philosophic advocacy of 'postmodernism' as a doctrine is surely Jean-François Lyotard's, who defines it as a principle of 'incredulity towards grand narratives'.[6] Conversely, then, let's define 'modernity' as *any form of organization driven by grand-narrative-fuelled hope*. In my book I attempted to develop a grand narrative account of the whole history of grand narrative, as a genre: essentially understood as a series of contributory impulses, evolving, by trial and error, towards a proper appreciation of the solidarity of the shaken. And what emerged was the story of three successive 'modernities', based upon three distinct species of grand narrative.

The story begins with the speech of the first Christian martyr, St Stephen, at his trial before the High Priest in Jerusalem, in Acts 7. Grand narrative is an invention of Christianity, and this is the very earliest reported example. Every grand narrative has what one might call its 'carrier community': the missionary community that spreads it, and whose sense of vocation it serves to define. What Stephen and his innumerable Christian successors represent is grand narrative with a particular religious group as its exclusive carrier community. And later on one finds the same general species of grand narrative also developing within the alternative matrix of Islam. Here, if you like, we have the stage of *first modernity*. In both the Christian-confessional and the Islamic-confessional matrices one can undoubtedly see some intimations of the solidarity of the shaken arising. But what's absent at this stage is any proper way of distinguishing it from the more ideological forms of solidarity between Christian and Christian, simply as such, or between Muslim and Muslim, simply as such.

Then, from the time of the Enlightenment onwards a second species of grand narrative begins to appear, generating what I call *second modernity*. This is grand narrative with quite a different sort of carrier community: elites self-defined in secular terms. Out of the French Revolution, for instance, there emerges the historic vision of the Marquis de Condorcet. By way of German radical alternative: the Enlightenment-apocalyptic doctrine of Fichte. And, in recoil from Fichte: that great masterpiece of the genre, the far more theologically open, and moderate, work of Hegel. In its mature form, this second species comes to frame the ideology of 'progressive' political parties. On the one hand, there's the broad category of liberal-reformist 'Whig history' and, on the other, the various forms of socialist grand narrative – above all, Marxism. All of these post-Enlightenment phenomena belong to projects for changing the world through the agency of the secular state. The carrier communities, in each case, are elites aspiring to gain direct governmental control of states, in order to impose the reforms they advocate. Again, no doubt there's very often been a considerable element of the solidarity of the shaken feeding into these projects. But the quest involved for governmental power means that this is forever being overlaid, and eventually suppressed, by the strategic demands of 'political realism'.

'Postmodernism', in Lyotard's sense of that term, is, first and foremost, a sense of 'incredulity' towards that secular species of grand narrative, the basis of second modernity. Lyotard himself was once a believer in Marxism. His becoming a 'postmodernist' actually reflects his loss of faith in one particular grand narrative, the Marxist one, a loss of faith that he's then generalized. And the late twentieth-century vogue for 'postmodernism', as a whole, was very largely a symptom of left-wing intellectuals' sense of bereavement on losing faith in Marx. However, to reject the entire *genre* of grand narrative, as a thinking-through of hope, because of problems affecting only one *form* of it does seem to be a somewhat extravagant overreaction! The failings of Marxist grand narrative are the failings of Marxism, not of grand narrative. They derive from the ultimate impossibility of reconciling the Marxist propaganda project with the solidarity of the shaken.

This actual phrase, 'solidarity of the shaken', was in fact coined by the Czech philosopher Jan Patočka.[7] Patočka was himself the founder of a public conscience movement, namely, the Charter 77 campaign for freedom of speech and other basic human rights in Communist Czechoslovakia; he co-founded Charter 77 with Václav Havel. Charter 77 was not least – one might well say – a solidarity movement seeking to defend the cultural space required for publicly airing the crucial Question, in all its various manifestations. So it battled against a regime that simply sought to suppress that Question's always subversive, shaking-open power by preventing its public expression, or the public expression of any thinking infused with it, anywhere. The movement had no other ideological basis apart from its commitment to the opening-up of public conversation. It wasn't aiming to overthrow and replace the regime, a prospect that at the time scarcely seemed feasible. Yet it united people with the otherwise most diverse views on religion and politics. In this, it resembled all sorts of other public conscience movements.

Mightn't such movements in general, then, become the carrier communities for yet another species of grand narrative: altogether more decisively oriented towards the solidarity of the shaken than those of either first or second modernity? My book was a plea for this possibility. In that sense, it was an attempt to imagine a *'third modernity'*.

Not all forms of grand narrative theory are bound up with predictions of the future. For example, Hegel's isn't. And Hegel's principled reticence in this regard is no doubt well advised. Not only are such predictions unscientific. More importantly, they serve no purpose proper to the solidarity of the shaken. For, after all, the solidarity of the shaken is a form of solidarity based upon a shared experience of having already been shaken open by the crucial Question, in whatever way. In itself, this has nothing to do with any shared assurance of future triumph. The main purpose of predictive grand narrat- ive is to help boost the morale of actual or aspirant ruling elites. Francis Fukuyama's famous book, *The End of History and the Last Man*, is a fine specimen of such argument encouraging an already established set of elites, in this case those of con- temporary American-style free-market democracy.[8] Fukuyama develops an elegant narrative argument basically designed to reassure these elites. In effect he's saying, 'History decrees that the sort of regime you represent will last for ever.' Fichte and Marx, in contrast, both in their different ways develop nar- rative arguments to encourage up-and-coming revolutionary elites. Their message, in effect, is, 'History decrees that after all your cause will prevail.' Fukuyama's theory, to be sure, is less sinister, in that it's explicitly anti-totalitarian.[9] But even this most liberal form of grand-narrative-based prediction still has nothing to do with the solidarity of the shaken. For my part, therefore, I make no predictions. But I simply want to insist on the sheer scale of the unprecedented new *opportunity* now opening up for Christian theology; which few people yet seem fully to appreciate.

The 'solidarity of the shaken' is a late twentieth-century concept originating out of the experience of public conscience movements. But, as I've said, it seems to me very closely akin to what Jesus, in the Synoptic Gospels, calls the 'kingdom of God', or the 'kingdom of heaven'. Although emerging in such a different context, it's basically the same phenomenon. The advent of the kingdom of God elicits a decisive move 'beyond good and evil', as defined by the mere moral conventionality of the herd – and so it generates the solidarity of the shaken. Addressing his disciples in the fourth Gospel, Jesus opens up the future:

> I still have many things to say to you, but you cannot bear them now. When the Spirit of truth comes, he will guide you into all the truth. (John 16.12–13)

The history of the Holy Spirit is surely the history of the inspiration of the kingdom of God. But, in retrospect, one may also see it as the history of the solidarity of the shaken. Where's the Holy Spirit at work in the world today? I'd answer that this work is most strikingly apparent in the emergent partnership between secular public conscience movements and religious traditions of every kind. For every religious tradition has at least some potential to become an enduring vessel for the solidarity of the shaken. And, again, it's in the ethos of public conscience movements that the solidarity of the shaken comes to its most direct expression.

Clearly, that ethos does also have its strategic weaknesses: public conscience movements tend to be shallow rooted, with their membership confined to the better-educated classes. Also, they're often quite ephemeral. In both these regards, they lack just what religious traditions are uniquely well equipped to supply.

In fact, Charter 77 itself exemplified both these weaknesses. The Chartist movement lasted some 12 years. For a while it became the focus for a whole, extraordinarily lively counter-culture. During that period the decayed grandeur of Communist Prague was home to two worlds. On top: the official world of sulky bureaucracy, vacuous speeches, half-hearted displays of kitsch propaganda. But underneath: the defiant, magnificently free-spirited world of the Chartists. Of course, this was before the days of the word processor. And, deprived of access to printing presses, or even photocopiers, in ill-lit apartments throughout the city people sat at typewriters, using inter-leafed carbon paper to hand-produce multiple copies of Chartist literature. At long last, though, there came what, at the outset, no one had anticipated, the sudden change in the political weather at the end of 1989. When the official world collapsed, the other world, which had been held so tightly together by resistance to it, burst apart. The Chartist playwright, Václav Havel, looking rather uncomfortable in a smart suit, was installed by public acclaim in the Castle, as President. Ordinary multiparty democratic politics began again. Before long the city was a major, glitzy tourist destination. Now that its original context had vanished, the spirit of the Chartists also – I suppose, inevitably – evaporated.

The meaning of the kingdom of God is revealed in the symbolic spectacle of a man crucified. Every serious experience of oppression is also a potential moment of truth. For it's an encounter with divine judgement: did you resist, or didn't you? The more intense this encounter is, the more it tends to propel one 'beyond' merely banal, conventional notions of 'good and evil'. To me, the basic moral of the story of Charter 77 is that we need to learn how to bottle something of the spirit that, for a brief while, gushed up there, under such great pressure, and preserve it in the altogether more durable form of a religious tradition.

Charter 77 embodied that spirit with singular intensity. Yet, it's a spirit that's also present in all sorts of other similarly constituted movements today: calling the natural inertia of things into question. And wherever it appears – this urgent register of the 'brokenness' in the 'broken middle' of our world – we surely need to recognize it as the working of the Holy Spirit, knock-knock-knocking at the doors of the Church, now, in new ways. Never before, as a result, has there been such a chance of clarity, to distinguish what amplifies, from what inhibits the asking of the crucial Question. Never before!

So much depends on how the Church represents its own history to itself, liturgically; and hence to the world, evangelistically. Get it wrong, and our whole proclamation of the gospel is corrupted.

The story of the Church in 'first modernity' is of a little, powerless community rising to great power, thanks to the patronage of emperors and kings; then justifying that power by appeal to the supposedly unambiguous sheer truth-as-correctness of the gospel. Whereas, by contrast, the proper claims of truth-as-openness – which to the rulers of the Church appeared all too subversive – were more or less suppressed. Thus, to begin with, theology tended to be altogether overwhelmed by the ideological self-interest of the Church institution. At least, later on, with the eventual emergence of 'second modernity', out of the Enlightenment, this ideological arrogance did begin to be rolled back. The *momentum*, at that point, shifted. But there still remains a powerful impulse, also within 'second modernity', to misconceive faith, confusing it with mere loyal adherence to a 'Christian' project of social control: 'Christian Democracy' or 'Christian Socialism'.

Only insofar as we reach 'third modernity' – if indeed our corporate self-understanding ever can reach so far – will the Church, once and for all, begin to grasp the real truth of God-as-Questioner for what in fact it is. *Not until then will we arrive at the possibility of a Church fundamentally dedicated to the asking of the crucial Question, and to nothing else.*

3

Beyond Liberal Theology

Two experiments: the Liberal and the Charismatic

Richard Dawkins, who is always good for a provocative quote, at one point cites a passage he finds in the *Catholic Encyclopedia*, from the third-century theologian St Gregory the Miracle Worker, intended to summarize the orthodox doctrine of the Trinity. And comments:

> Whatever miracles may have earned St Gregory his nickname, they were not miracles of honest lucidity. His words convey the characteristically obscurantist flavour of theology, which – unlike science or most other branches of human scholarship – has not moved on in eighteen centuries.[1]

However, theology has in fact surely 'moved on', over that period, at least as much as any other discipline of the humanities! Again, we just need to be clear what 'moving on' means here.

What does it mean for theology to 'move on'? My answer would be that, above all, it is by developing new modes of increasingly explicit *attunement* to the crucial Question: accentuating its power to disturb and dislodge rigid prejudice.[2] Every Church tradition, or family of traditions, needs essentially to be assessed as a series of experiments to that end.

To me, as a Church of England priest at the beginning of the second millennium, the current background to the theological scene appears largely shaped by two great processes of ongoing experiment – both of which are primarily Protestant, although with Roman Catholic echoes. And both of which were more or less inaugurated in the eighteenth century. One is the scholarly enterprise of *Liberal Theology*. By far the greater part of academic theology over the past two centuries or more has arisen out of the interplay between Liberal Theology and its conservative critics. While the other (less academic) is the *Charismatic Movement*: using the term 'Charismatic' here, in a broad sense, to include Pentecostalism along with other related phenomena.

Let's consider these two phenomena side by side. For, in a sense, they're balancing opposites.

How shall we assess their achievements? An ideal Church culture would surely include a good mix of the following three primary elements.

1 *Free-spirited intellectuality.* By this I mean an attunement to the crucial Question framed in terms of sophisticated argument. Here we have what Liberal Theology prioritizes. For it's the theology of free-spirited intellectuals, systematically relating 'Why am I what I am? What am I called to become?' to a scholarly analysis of why we, the Christian community as a whole, are what we are, how the Church has arrived at its present position and how it might change.
2 *Eloquent enthusiasm.* In other words: an attunement to the crucial Question framed in terms of intense emotional self-expression. This is what the Charismatic Movement prioritizes, as it presses home the life-transforming potential of 'Why am I what I am? What am I called to become?' with a truly impassioned yearning for better things.
3 *Sacramental inclusiveness.* Or an attunement to the crucial Question framed in terms of the sheer unconditional generosity of divine love. In particular: its complete independence of people's intellectual or emotive skills. I call this 'sacramental' inasmuch as a 'sacrament' is a ritual understood to possess objective validity quite regardless of either the intelligence

or the immediate show of fervour that its participants bring to it. For the specifically theological purpose of sacraments is to draw together, into a potential conversation space, all sorts.

Both Liberal Theology and the Charismatic Movement emphasize just one of the three elements. Consider the two of them side by side – *how they've fallen apart from one another* – and, in my view, you immediately see the fundamental importance of the third sort of emphasis, which ought to hold them together. The importance of that third principle is highlighted by the unfortunate deficiency, in each of these two contexts, of a proper appreciation of it.

Thus, each element, to the extent that it's cut off from the other two, grows increasingly ambiguous. Liberal Theology, as a disciplined cultivation of free-spirited intellectuality, is partly an intimation of the solidarity of the shaken: one becomes a Liberal theologian because one's been shaken open by the challenge of the crucial Question, academically conceived, and because one's looking for like-minded academic allies. But at the same time this remains a conversation-process confined to a particular social class. One can only participate in it if one's reasonably well educated. A commitment to Liberal Theology immediately leads to conflict with those others in the Church who are less well educated, or at any rate less confident in their education, and therefore more inclined to take everything in Church tradition simply at its face value. The Liberal theologian, as such – looking beyond the face value of the tradition so as to develop its capacity, intellectually, to evoke the crucial Question – is inclined to be impatient with this. However, that impatience is highly ambiguous. It isn't just the solidarity of the shaken that emerges here. But it may, at any rate, also be seen as the all-too-natural arrogance of a privileged social class, chafing at the constraints of authentically 'catholic' church life.

The Charismatic Movement, meanwhile, is also partly an intimation of the solidarity of the shaken, albeit in quite a different way. For, again, one becomes a charismatic Christian because one's been shaken open by the challenge of the crucial Question – in this case, the crucial Question experienced with an intense, yearning enthusiasm – and because one's looking for like-minded allies. But, just as in the opposite case of Liberal Theology, the intimation of the solidarity of the shaken here immediately tends to get mixed up with other impulses that are bound up with class conflict. From the days of John Wesley onwards, the Charismatic Movement has primarily appealed to the downtrodden, as a path of defiant self-respect; it's been a rival to more political movements of protest. But then its theology has, therefore, typically evolved as a strategy for keeping privileged intellectuals *out*. This is surely why the theology of the post-Wesleyan Charismatic Movement has always tended to be fundamentalist. To be fair-minded towards Charismatic fundamentalism, one needs to register it as a desperate form of protest against intellectual arrogance, by those who know no way of confronting such arrogance on its own territory.

Both Liberal Theology and the Charismatic Movement carry within them sparks of the solidarity of the shaken. But when one sees how these two movements have fallen apart into such complete theological opposition to one another, one also sees how much they've both, at the same time, been shaped by other, class-ideological impulses. Liberal Theology is liable to mix the solidarity of the shaken with the snobbish self-assertion of intellectuals as a privileged class; the Charismatic Movement tends to mix the solidarity of the shaken with the propaganda of brilliant populist showmen. The rivalry between intellectuals and showmen drives the two movements apart.

Only a Church truly faithful to the third principle, of sacramental inclusiveness, can inspire genuine loyalty on the part of both intellectuals and non-intellectuals alike, thereby drawing the privileged and the downtrodden together into authentic, mutually respectful conversation. Let the charismatic showmen not give up on their flair for the theatrical – it can certainly help people to connect with the true drama of faith, as a more than merely intellectual response to the crucial Question. But let them clearly recognize the associated dangers of narrow-mindedness. And let the liberal-minded intellectuals, likewise, not suppress their critical intelligence, but nevertheless resist the associated temptations of impatience. Let both acknowledge the sheer unconditional generosity of God's love for all, regardless of people's religious tastes and aptitudes.

To be sure, a form of church life that only emphasizes the third principle, that of sacramental inclusiveness – to the detriment of free-spirited intellectuality and eloquent enthusiasm – will also tend to lapse into its own species of ambiguity. In this case, the solidarity of the shaken merges into mere solidarity among neighbours – with a wrapping of quite uncritical, essentially sentimental, universal benevolence. At its worst, the result is nothing but the most unthinking sort of cosy folk religion. But sacramental inclusiveness nevertheless surely is a necessary part of the ideal mix, as it serves to hold free-spirited intellectuality together with eloquent enthusiasm, in a unified whole-community attunement to the crucial Question.

The three great achievements of the Liberals

I myself come from the world of Liberal Theology. To adopt Martin Luther's phrase, that's the particular 'Babylonian captivity of the Church' I'm seeking to escape. However, the original Babylonian captivity of the people of Israel wasn't only a disaster. It was also providential, rendering possible the breakthrough insights of Deutero-Isaiah. And my view of Liberal Theology remains ambivalent.

Liberal Theology has accomplished at least three great things. It's reconnected, as never before, with the historic humanity of Jesus; it's uncovered, as never before, the true nature of the Bible as the literature of a conversation; and it's honoured, as never before, the indwelling of God within each human individual's individuality as such.

Thus:

1 *Reconnecting with the historic humanity of Jesus*
The so-called 'quest for the historical Jesus' originates within the world of Liberal Theology. As a Liberal project, the 'quest' is essentially an attempt to reconnect with Jesus as proclaimer of the 'kingdom of God'. That's to say, with his initial strategy for pressing home the crucial Question, at its most urgent and purest – not yet contaminated by any taint of Church ideology.

Some ultra-Liberals have, indeed, sought to base everything on this. Leo Tolstoy is one very striking example. More recently, Don Cupitt is another.[3] However, the results of the 'quest' have also complicated matters, in ways that seem to render that strategy somewhat problematic. The difficulties first really came to the surface in that great mid-nineteenth-century classic, David Friedrich Strauss's *Life of Jesus*.[4] For Strauss, in this pioneering, free-spirited work, opts very much to emphasize those aspects of Jesus' world-view that no amount of interpretation can quite make fit with the ethos of modern theological Liberalism: the apocalyptic urgency of his preaching, with its anticipation of an imminent end to the world. Later, too, Johannes Weiss and Albert Schweitzer in particular accentuated the same aspect of the matter still further. Maybe they did so to excess. And yet the problem still remains for any form of Liberalism, as such, intent on claiming the historic Jesus for itself.

2 *Comprehending the Bible as a conversation*
At the same time classic Liberal Theology also opened up the method of reading the Bible that Strauss's tutor, and later friend, Ferdinand Christian Baur dubbed '*tendency criticism*'.[5]

The recitation of the Qur'an, or of the Torah, is a sacramental act. Christianity has other sacraments, and ideally therefore the Christian Bible is set free to play another role, not quite so untouchably sacrosanct. Its essential truth surely lies in the exemplary human openness it displays to God's questioning. Truth-as-openness: again, this is a quality of conversation. And the Bible initiates us into the great conversation-process of Christian theology, not least by virtue of the way in which it is itself already the literature of a conversation, involving such a wide variety of different human voices, in both the foreground and the background of its texts. God's questioning insinuates itself, by infection, through the conversational interplay of these texts, into the force field of dialectically evolving ideas that they generate. The devotees of God as Divine Despot are reluctant to acknowledge this: *they'd* much rather pretend that the Bible speaks with a single voice, that of the Divine Despot himself, their God, who's not a questioner at all but a dictator. But Baur and his allies, the so-called Tübingen School of biblical interpretation, set themselves, in pioneering fashion, systematically to dispel that illusion, by focusing above all on the different basic polemic interests, or 'tendencies', of the various biblical authors, and on the intra-communal struggles that gave rise to their work. Divine Despot theology is forever abstracting biblical texts from their original context in a human conversation. 'Tendency criticism' does the opposite. One might describe it as the application of X-ray and ultrasound scanning to the body of the Bible, so as to observe and comprehend the organic workings, in it, of the Holy Spirit, through the conversations of the early Church.

And this has arguably produced rather more solid results, long term, than the 'quest for the historical Jesus', even though the specific exegetical theory advanced by the original Tübingen School has now in fact been refuted in almost all its details. Baur focused on the conflict between Paul, as advocate of the freest possible Christian evangelistic approach to Gentiles, and his 'Petrine' opponents, for whom Gentile converts first needed to become in the fullest possible sense Jews. Nowadays, it's generally accepted that he exaggerated both the scope and the duration of the conflict between these two 'tendencies'.[6] Never mind. There are a great many other more or less concealed 'tendency'-conflicts discernible within the biblical texts; it's just that 'tendency criticism' now takes other, more nuanced forms. The errors of the Tübingen School were the necessary experiments of a pioneer movement, testing the limits of the possible. But the basic *methodological* principle that these scholars introduced surely is valid.

3 *Honouring individuality*

And then, underlying both the 'quest for the historical Jesus' and 'tendency criticism', there is in Liberal Theology a great affirmation of free-spirited individuality. This appears, up to a point, in Friedrich Schleiermacher's pioneering concern with the phenomenology of individual 'religious experience', and his attempt to ground the whole enterprise of theology on that basis. But its most radical expression is in G. W. F. Hegel's philosophic critique of Divine Despot theology. Both Strauss and Baur are generally (if rather loosely) reckoned to be 'Hegelian' thinkers.

Hegel diagnoses Divine Despot theology as a symptom of what he calls the '*Unhappy Consciousness*'.[7] But the 'Unhappy Consciousness' is a universal phenomenon, to be found in every cultural context, not only in monotheistic religion. To some extent, it's something from which we all of us suffer. In fact, it's simply Hegel's general name for *whatever*, within the mind, serves to suppress, or inhibit, our response to the crucial Question. Although he calls it a form of 'consciousness', it's essentially *un*-conscious of its true misery; it must be, otherwise that misery would be intolerable. He analyses it as an internally divided state of mind, a form of inner servitude, a self-fooling condition.

Deep down, the objective 'unhappiness' of the 'Unhappy Consciousness' consists in an essential lack of self-confidence, on the part of the individual as an individual. To respond to the crucial Question is to confront the prevailing prejudices of one's own social world. But these prejudices are of course also lodged within one's own mind. There, they form a sort of sub-self, which Hegel terms the 'Unchangeable'. This is set over against the potentially Questioning sub-self, the 'Changeable'. The 'Unhappy Consciousness' is essentially the despotic rule, within the individual psyche, of the 'Unchangeable' over the 'Changeable'. Here, then, the 'Unchangeable' seeks to cow the 'Changeable' into submission: 'By what right do you presume to question the established ways that you've been taught? You have no right!' And in monotheistic cultures this further becomes, 'Who are you, miserable sinner that you are, to challenge the Lord God?'

But monotheism *may*, equally, express liberation from the 'Unhappy Consciousness'. And that in fact is how Hegel understands the origins of Christian faith in the Incarnation. So, as he sees it, God 'descending from heaven' to become incarnate in Christ is essentially a symbolic representation of God breaking free from the theological self-projection of the 'Unhappy Consciousness'. The tyranny of the 'Unhappy Consciousness' involves a radical devaluation of human individuality: 'Who am I, a mere individual, to question the given order?' In its monotheistic form, therefore, it accentuates the infinite distance between the human individual and God – that is, 'God' understood as the amplified voice of the 'Unchangeable' – in order to reinforce that attitude of contempt. Christian faith, however, sees God made manifest precisely in the form of a human individual. The vast distance between God and the human individual that the 'Unhappy Consciousness' posits has been symbolically annihilated. God, here, is revealed incarnate in an historic human individual, not a mythic one; a very ordinary one in social status, not an emperor, not a king, in the worldly sense; and, moreover, a dissident, a crucified dissident – this simply underlines the same point. For, again, nothing could more vividly symbolize the contempt of repressive rulers for human individuality, their lack of respect for its intrinsic rights, than the act of crucifixion. And nothing, therefore, could more vividly symbolize the overthrow of that attitude than the resurrection of a crucified individual.

The 'Unhappy Consciousness' is irrepressible. It fights back. The truth of Christian faith, for Hegel, essentially consists in its poetic power to express the overthrow of this mentality. Yet, liberation from the 'Unhappy Consciousness' is neither dependent on 'correct' Christian faith nor at all guaranteed by it, even at its most sincere. Hegel's original discussion of the 'Unhappy Consciousness' is actually full of allusive reference to the various ways in which this mentality reappears within Christianity. It's able to reappear there because of the intrinsic ambiguity of all religious 'picture thinking'. Only philosophy can, in the end, disentangle that ambiguity, he argues: philosophy pointing beyond the 'correct' formulas of faith to how it's *appropriated*. The 'Unhappy Consciousness' may appropriate Christian faith in a perfectly orthodox way, but, no matter how orthodox its understanding, it empties it of any real rationale. It reduces faith to a matter of quite arbitrary assertion.

Indeed, Hegel is undoubtedly right: everything depends upon how the revelation of God-within-Christ is appropriated; to what extent, in actual practice, God's indwelling within Christ is taken to represent God's indwelling within every individual soul. Or how far, in other words, it's understood as a direct defiance of the 'Unhappy Consciousness', and hence as a truly decisive symbolic affirmation of *the confidence to question*.

He was the first ever thinker of the Christian tradition to see *this* conflict as the absolutely central issue, on which the whole truth of Christian theology depends. Here, he claimed, the history of Christian thought had reached a real breakthrough moment. In his larger 'philosophy of Spirit' he develops a history of 'Spirit', that is, the impulse to perfect truth-as-openness, struggling towards true self-awareness. It's a vast, many layered grand narrative, bringing together history of religion, history of art and history of philosophy with political history. But right at its heart is the fresh take that he's proposing, on the Christian gospel. All the rest, in the end, is elaborate background to that. Hegel had hoped it would shortly become part of the general consensus of Christian theologians. Alas, it hasn't, yet. It surely should.

And yet, something's missing . . .

Hitherto, within the Church, Liberal Theology has for the most part been criticized – in somewhat sweeping (Augustinian) fashion – on the broad grounds of its not being critical enough of modern 'secular' culture, as a whole. Such is the argument, for instance, of Karl Barth, Hans Urs von Balthasar and all their many allies; of Herman Dooyeweerd; of Hans Frei and George Lindbeck; and of the Radical Orthodoxy group today.

This very general critique is arguably fair enough when applied to the sort of Liberal Theology stemming from Schleiermacher, theological genius though Schleiermacher undoubtedly was. There's minimal real critique of secular modernity in that tradition. Schleiermacher gives such absolute priority to apologetics, addressing Christianity's 'cultured despisers', that is, alienated secular modern intellectuals, and basically seeking to make it as *easy* as possible for them to return to the Church's fold. So he presents them with the challenge of faith as requiring only a minimum shift in moral attitude, just a renewed respect for individual 'religious experience', that is, a cultivated Romantic liking for certain forms of religious sentiment, with such sentiment, in effect, served up as sauce to add a piquant flavour to modernity.

And much the same attitude to modernity also seems to underlie Baur's approach to Church history, or that of other Liberals such as Harnack after him. The story they tell is one of quite uncomplicated general progress, culminating in the enlightened religious outlook of Liberal academics like Baur or Harnack themselves.

The case of Hegel is, in fact, considerably more complex. He too of course tells a story of progress. But he compares the opportunity he sees in his own day, for fresh theological insight, to the opportunity, within the world of decadent Roman paganism, which originally made possible the rise of the early Church. This is a recurrent theme of his. The new opportunity, as he sees it, to a large extent lies in a condition of decadence: it's a matter of channelling the discontents to which that decadence gives rise. Hegel is fiercely critical of the early nineteenth-century cultural world in which he lived: he deplores the decay of any real sense of ethical community in his world, the class antagonisms, the proliferation of rootless, alienated intellectuals, prey to all manner of dangerous ideology. He's allergic, not least, to the new forms of often intensely antisemitic German nationalism that were, in that period, just beginning to emerge; and he's haunted by the still fresh memory of the French Revolutionary Terror. His general attitude to modernity was far more critical than that of Schleiermacher, in particular. The two men, colleagues at the University of Berlin, had a rather troubled relationship. From Hegel's point of view, Schleiermacher appeared far too uncritically predisposed to sympathize with every form of high-flown Romantic sentiment, simply as such, not only religious but also political. And so, not least, he failed to see the real danger of the new nationalism as Hegel saw it; unlike Hegel, he was seduced by its sentimental quality.[8]

In historical retrospect, of course, Hegel's altogether more critical attitude may well be said to have been vindicated. Nevertheless, there clearly *is* something out of kilter even in the Hegelian version of Liberal Theology. This is apparent, above all, in the way that he's been misunderstood.

The most egregious misinterpretation of Hegel's theology is that of Ludwig Feuerbach, who (in my view, bizarrely!) claims to be completing the Hegelian project, drawing it to its proper conclusion, by converting it into a form of atheistic humanism. Thus, Feuerbach, like Hegel, is preoccupied with the need to overcome Divine Despot theology. And, again like Hegel, he considers the Christian dogma of the Incarnation to be a key moment in the process of that overcoming. But there's a key difference. Whereas for Hegel, as we've seen, the individual divine-human figure of Christ, properly understood, symbolically represents *the infinite value of all human individuality as such*, for Feuerbach by contrast he represents *the infinite value of the species, Humanity, in general*. In stark contrast to Hegel, Feuerbach is a Promethean atheist, inasmuch as he wants to exalt 'Humanity' into the traditional role of God. For Hegel, Christ represents the more-or-less concealed indwelling of God within every individual human soul; for Feuerbach he represents the need to worship not God but 'Humanity' instead. This is surely a very ugly move, in the direction of a mere propaganda ideology. For what Feuerbach calls 'Humanity' is, in effect, just the projected self-image of a certain self-glorifying intellectual elite. He's appealing to those rootless intellectuals who feel least attachment to the various intermediate cultural identities occupying the space in between *'me, this particular individual'* and *'me, member of the human species thinking on behalf of the species as a whole'*. That's to say: those who feel alienated not only from any identity they might have within a religious community but also from their class identity, their ethnic identity, or their national identity. And he's effectively suggesting that such people should worship the corporate reflection of their alienated, cosmopolitan, intellectual selves. Feuerbach's 'Humanity' is no more than a projection: the projected mere vanity of angry outsider-intellectuals like himself.

Yet still he claimed to be a follower of Hegel. Somehow he managed to persuade not only himself but also a great many others that this is what Hegel, before him, had 'really' meant all along! According to Feuerbach, Hegel had only ever *pretended* to remain an orthodox Christian, out of fear and in order to keep his job. It was all just a ploy, to disguise his true doctrine. And that's what's so disturbing: the sheer fact that so many people have been ready to believe in such a fantastic travesty of an interpretation. Hegel represents Liberal Theology at its very best. Yet, *even here* something must be missing; some counterbalancing element that would have rendered Feuerbach's misreading, obtuse as it is, simply impossible.

Nothing could more disturbingly illustrate the constitutive one-sidedness of all Liberal Theology than the curious power and persistence of Feuerbach's grotesque misreading.

'Was ever another command so obeyed?'

The basic weakness of Liberal Theology, in general – I'm arguing – is that it colludes all too easily with the natural philosophic squeamishness of sophisticated intellectuals, when it comes to close communion with the unsophisticated.

Or, to say the same thing in other words: its problem is that *it isn't eucharistic enough*.

Thus, consider how the Eucharist functions as a channel for the crucial Question. Nothing could be simpler, in itself, than this Question: it requires absolutely no book learning to ask it of oneself, yet its depth of potential meaning is limitless. Infusing other questions, everywhere – and so expressed in a myriad of different forms – it's just what renders those other questions most deeply troubling.

The Eucharist symbolically enacts that dynamic, represents it in dramatic mode. Nothing could be simpler, in itself, than the central eucharistic act of eating consecrated bread and drinking consecrated wine. Yet, the depth of potential meaning in this act is limitless. And it can be adapted to every sort of context.

'Do this in remembrance of me,' says Jesus. 'Was ever another command so obeyed?' asks Dom Gregory Dix, in a beautiful passage.

For century after century, spreading slowly to every continent and country and among every race on earth, this action has been done, in every conceivable human circumstance, for every conceivable human need from infancy and before it to extreme old age and after it, from the pinnacles of earthly greatness to the refuge of fugitives in the caves and dens of the earth. Men have found no better thing than this to do for kings at their crowning and for criminals going to the scaffold; for armies in triumph or for a bride and bridegroom in a little country church; for the proclamation of a dogma or for a good crop of wheat; for the wisdom of the Parliament of a mighty nation or for a sick old woman afraid to die; for a school-boy sitting an examination or for Columbus setting out to discover America; for the famine of whole provinces or for the soul of a dead lover; in thankfulness because my father did not die of pneumonia; for a village headman much tempted to return to fetich because the yams had failed; because the Turk was at the gates of Vienna; for the repentance of Margaret; for the settlement of a strike; for a son for a barren woman; for Captain so-and-so, wounded and prisoner of war; while the lions roared in the nearby amphitheatre; on the beach at Dunkirk; while the hiss of scythes in the thick June grass came faintly through the windows of the church; tremulously, by an old monk on the fiftieth anniversary of his vows; furtively, by an exiled bishop who had hewn timber all day in a prison camp near Murmansk; gorgeously, for the canonisation of St Joan of Arc – one could fill many pages with the reasons why men have done this, and not tell a hundredth part of them. And best of all, week by week and month by month, on a hundred thousand successive Sundays, faithfully, unfailingly, across all the parishes of christendom, the pastors have done this just to *make* the *plebs sancta Dei* – the holy common people of God.[9]

But in order fully to participate in the holy *plebs* of God – a conversation space from which, so far as possible, *nobody* is excluded – one must, first of all, give up any desire of belonging to a sacred community of the right-minded. Even according to the genuinely most enlightened, 'liberal' understanding of right-mindedness! The true Church is a Church of the 'broken middle': of the middle by virtue of its openness in every direction, all God-blocking delusions of right-minded corporate innocence therefore broken.

If humanity is to cope at all with its various vast impending crises, we're surely going to need, not least, the unique sheer moral energy of such broken-middle, plebeian religion. Not suppressing difference, but nonetheless, come what may, helping hold us fast, educated and uneducated alike, in consultation together.

4

Beyond baptism-and-confirmation

The symbolic rightness of infant baptism

And now: two basic *organizational* questions about what it would mean for a Church to be ideally dedicated to the crucial Question: (1) what demands such a Church would make upon its members, as such; and (2) how it would build towards a global communion.

Two questions. One, so to speak, with regard to domestic policy, the other having to do with foreign policy. The second question is of course especially pressing in the current Anglican context. However, let's begin in this chapter with the first, saving the second for Chapter 5.

I grew up in a Church of England culture where Church membership was largely equated with a not very demanding sort of respectability. But, again, what does the crucial Question do to conventional notions of respectability, that is, herd-morality notions of 'good and evil'? It dissolves their authority. Faith, as an exposure to this Question, sweeps away the rival pretensions of any religious respectability-code directly to embody the highest ideal. So Paul, the first Christian theologian, subordinates 'law', meaning religion as respectability-code, to 'grace', the working of faith. 'What then?' he asks. 'Should we sin because we are not under law but under grace? By no means!' (Romans 6.15). It isn't that faith *necessarily* means repudiating the dictates of respectability. Paul is no lover of scandal, for the mere thrill's sake. Nevertheless, faith, as he understands it, does at any rate mean entertaining the possibility that, in some ways, respectability's notion of 'sin' may itself be a notion infected with sin. The first Christians opted for faith against respectability: Jews repudiating Jewish respectability, Gentiles repudiating Gentile respectability. In the Pastoral Epistles we can see a new respectability-code arising, this time a Christian one. But that's a later development. Writing to the church in Rome, Paul is simply intent on carving out new space for the crucial Question, with the crucified and resurrected Christ, representing God, as Questioner.

Nor does this principle only apply to the maximum of Church membership, the higher levels of sanctity. It also applies to the minimum. True sanctity isn't just a maximum of ultra-respectability, conventional morality topped up with extra turbo-charged energy. And no one, either, is properly excluded from full membership of the Church because they fail to meet some basic minimum respectability requirement. *This, I take it, is why we baptize infants.*

Thus, to be respectable is to know how to behave – respectability, in that sense, is the opposite of being infantile. But how then are the earnest advocates of Christian respectability to make sense of what Jesus says? 'Let the little children come to me; do not stop them . . . Truly I tell you, whoever does not receive the kingdom of God as a little child will never enter it' (Mark 10.14–15). The grace of faith, it seems, clears away the adult self preoccupied with respectability. It does so to make room for another, quite different sort of adult self, one that's still opened up to fresh moral insight the way a child is, namely, a devotee of the crucial Question. One who's capable of looking beyond the demands of respectability, to the altogether more troubling, because not yet codified, not yet learnt, demands of perfect justice, perfect love. In general, whenever the Church incorporates new members into itself, through the ritual of baptism, this is an occasion for it, symbolically, to represent itself to itself. And when, in particular, we baptize infants, then by that very act we're affirming that the Church is something altogether more than just a project for reinforcing standard adult roles. Far rather, it suggests, the Church is meant to be the creation of an open conversation space, a space for simple Honesty, in the 'broken middle', where the false protection offered by respectability has broken down. The baptized infant, not yet socialized, represents the future chance of unpredictable fresh stirrings of the Holy Spirit – all kinds of fresh insight – who knows what? And as it welcomes its new member, the Church, in principle, also welcomes that chance.

Moreover, the practice of infant baptism also seems to affirm that the conversation within this space will be governed by a profoundly *egalitarian* ethos. Here, it says, everyone's interests count equally: look, even an infant, in that sense, counts as equal to anyone else, in the order of the Church community! This is what I've called the 'principle of sacramental inclusiveness' (see p. 53). Understood in these terms, the proper sacramental nature of all baptism actually appears at its clearest in the baptism of infants. Again, neither Liberal Theology nor the Charismatic Movement is egalitarian enough: Liberal Theology fails adequately to challenge the natural dominance of the better educated, the Charismatic Movement fails adequately to challenge the natural dominance of those who are most skilled in the public expression of emotion. At the deepest level, infant baptism needs to be interpreted as a ritual act of resistance against the temptations inherent in both sorts of dominance, insofar as they tend to become oppressive of those who are less well educated, or less skilled in self-expression. So it affirms God's infinite, unconditional love for all, quite regardless of their accomplishments. God infinitely and unconditionally loves even this child, who has no accomplishments whatsoever of which to boast. The very act of baptizing an infant speaks eloquently of love that isn't a reward, but is all gift; love that is the pure antithesis, therefore, to any sort of manipulation; that is sheer tenderness.

This is beautiful.

And yet, then – look: we've messed it up! For, surely, the authentic sacramental power of infant baptism lies in its representing full admission into Church membership. Everything here, in symbolic terms, depends upon the child's inaugurated membership in the Church being both unconditional and complete. However, it turns out that (whatever we may say to the contrary) in actual Church of England practice the baptized infant is no more than a *half*-member of the Church. The way we've organized things, you only become a full member when – at some later age, and *after some sort of training* – you're confirmed, by the laying-on of a bishop's hands. Baptism, our tradition insists, needs to be 'completed' by confirmation, and until that's happened, still in most Church of England churches (although thank God things are now beginning to change) you're not entitled to receive the bread and wine of the Eucharist. That's to say, when it comes to the primary symbolic act that signifies ongoing Church membership, you remain symbolically excluded. The training required for confirmation may be pretty perfunctory, but even so the symbolic message is clear enough. Full membership is conditional on that training. After all, what baptism represents here is no unconditional offer of full belonging, to reflect the unconditional gift of divine love. And, hence, it can scarcely be said to be a pure showing-forth of 'grace'. Instead, it's become a promissory work of 'law'. The sheer generosity of its underlying sacramental truth has been overlaid with anxious ecclesiastical nagging: 'Godparents, this is your duty, baptism ought to lead to confirmation, don't forget . . .' And the authentic testimony of faith begins to disappear into that nagging.

I think that the separation of first communion from baptism is a quite basic theological mistake. It shows us a Church perhaps mistrusting the sheer ease and generosity of divine *agapē*, symbolically pulling back from it. Or, at the very least, not wanting to give symbolic priority to this aspect of the matter, but letting other concerns overlay and conceal it.

71

Martin Luther in his day launched a great onslaught on respectability-code religion, invoking the authority of Paul against it, and setting out to establish a whole new Church on that basis. In the process, he repudiated the old mediaeval rite of confirmation. Nor did he personally want to replace it. But (alas!) the Reformation wasn't only an onslaught on respectability-religion. It was *also* a movement harnessing the pride of the literate laity – quite a different matter – and Luther, therefore, still didn't think it symbolically appropriate to admit children to communion without, first, putting them through a good bit of compulsory book learning, so as to affirm that pride. Therefore, he produced his own Catechism for the purpose. And then, in 1538, his colleague Martin Bucer drafted a scheme of Lutheran Church order for the state of Hesse, which did, after all, include a new confirmation rite. One way or another, all the most notable Reformers who subsequently, like Luther, continued to practise infant baptism followed Bucer's lead. Including, despite some initial misgivings, the Anglicans.

But, in opposition to the Old Reformation, the New Reformation I advocate would involve a complete break from the practice. The Eastern Orthodox churches manage perfectly well without it. For them, infant baptism, confirmation (or rather 'chrismation', the ancient rite of anointing with oil that in the West evolved into confirmation) and first communion are typically three parts of one and the same liturgical event. And, while it may have come about more by accident than design, it seems to me that, so far as this goes, the Orthodox have got it right.

A ritual celebration of wisdom?

But surely – it will be objected – we do need some sort of rite in which those baptized as infants can, once they're old enough, positively own their membership in the Church for themselves. Don't we?

Yes, we do. Only, what sort of 'owning' is required? What counts as 'old enough', for this purpose? And why on earth should having been through such a ritual be made a precondition for sharing in the Eucharist?

Suppose one was starting from scratch to devise an ideal regime of Christian initiation. On the one hand, the liturgy needs to communicate the absolutely unconditional nature of divine love. But, on the other hand, it *also* needs to communicate the infinitely restless proper orientation of faith towards the deepest wisdom. Both principles are vital; there's a basic requirement of balance here.

Two Greek terms capture this balance. In general, the progress of Truth is partly the work of *isothymia*: people's insistence on being recognized as the innate equal, in dignity, of other people, their sheer refusal therefore to be put down and silenced. And partly it's the work of *megalothymia*, people's ambition to be acknowledged in their achieved uniqueness, for the special insights that are most distinctively theirs.[1] Baptism *as a sacrament*, especially the baptism of infants, and the Eucharist *as a sacrament* are both of them, first and foremost, rituals of holy *isothymia*, that is, the spirited affirmation of equality. They symbolically enact the underlying equality of all God's children. However, we no doubt do also need encouraging rituals of holy *megalothymia*, the spirited affirmation of achieved individuality, to supplement them. My objection to the traditional Church of England rite of confirmation, and to other such rites in other churches, is simply that they're so inadequate for that second purpose.

The point is this. A celebration of holy *megalothymia* (the spirited affirmation of achieved individuality) would, in essence, be an invitation for each individual to consider his, or her, own God-given vocation in life, as something altogether more than just a matter of conventional role-play. It would be, precisely, the expression of a much deeper form of respect, for each individual's achieved individuality, than the ordinary respect we accord to 'respectability'. Not everyone has a dramatic, world-shaking vocation. But every adult has a vocation of some sort, to be set over against the mere passive drift of herd-morality – as also against the glamorous allure of the gang, or the mindless excitement of the mob. A celebration of holy *megalothymia* would, in the first instance, be an act of resistance against the mentalities of the mob, the gang and the herd.

How, though, can we at all seriously honour an individual vocation, in this sense, until it has, quite clearly, *emerged*? Every infant may also be said to have an individual vocation, hidden in the future; every adolescent may be said to have an individual vocation, just beginning to peep out. But it's only when one has become an adult that the actual shape of one's vocation begins to become truly visible – that's what 'adulthood', as a moral category, means. I agree: if we're going to baptize infants then we do need some sort of ritual supplement to baptism, in order also, concretely, to reflect upon what one might call the vocational implications of faith, towards which the liturgy of infant baptism can only gesture in the abstract. However, this is no argument for the traditional rite of confirmation! The traditional rite mostly involves the wrong age group. If we were serious about wanting to celebrate the proper owning of faith – and if it really was *faith* we had in mind, and not just a simple conformity to either one's parents' wishes or peer-group pressure – then we wouldn't have ended up with a rite like this. Not with one chiefly intended for young adolescents, and only for adults if, for some reason, they've missed out in adolescence.

The Baptists charge us with trivializing faith: failing to express, through our initiation rites, its full counter-cultural thrust. They're surely right. Nothing, in ritual terms, more vividly expresses our basic lack of corporate seriousness about the crucial Question, the real truth we're charged to communicate, than our practice in this regard.

In abandoning infant baptism, the Baptists have given up on half of what's required: the *isothymia* half. At least, though, their system makes some sense according to the other, the *megalothymia* half. The baptism of adults is, clearly, far more likely than the confirmation of adolescents to represent a serious act of commitment. But we by contrast, having traditionally made confirmation the gateway to first communion, have forever been impelled to lower the minimum age for confirmation because we've been embarrassed about excluding devout youngsters from communion. And the lower the age creeps, the less meaningful the rite becomes.

We've excluded young children from communion on the grounds that they lack the necessary 'understanding'. In my view, one of the most important things to understand about communion is that 'understanding' *isn't* a necessary prerequisite for meaningful participation.

Yet then it's suggested that young adolescents, or older children, *can* understand, in the operative sense. And so what exactly constitutes this crucial element of understanding that one's supposed to attain, more or less, around the age of puberty?

I was confirmed and received my first communion at the age of 14. As it happens, I was a rather devout teenager. One day I'd come across the word 'mysticism' in a book, and asked my parents what it meant. My mother pointed me towards Evelyn Underhill's classic work on the subject, and I found it inspiring.[2] Here, I felt, was true seriousness! I thought that maybe I'd grow up to become a monk. And I took to searching through second-hand bookshops for the great writings of the Christian mystical tradition, as identified by Evelyn Underhill in the historical appendix to her study. Before long I had quite a collection. I practised contemplative prayer; vague adolescent *megalothymia* blazed within me, in the most sanctified form. You might well think that for such a child confirmation would indeed have been a big deal. However, it wasn't. The preparation course was conscientiously run, warm, humorous. I remember that. Nevertheless, the fact is that when I search my memory today the whole actual ceremony itself has vanished. Doubtless it was an event of great mediaeval splendour, shafts of sunlight falling through the stained-glass windows, organ music crashing and surging around soft moments of stillness, the bishop doing his best to make us all feel valued. So I imagine. But no – nothing at all! Nothing's registered. I was too young. In retrospect it seems clear to me that, for all my reading and inner turmoil, I didn't yet have enough to bring to the event, that was all of my own, to make it a truly meaningful, and therefore memorable, moment of lifelong commitment.

Confirmation, of course, is meant to be an occasion for those who were baptized as infants to reiterate, this time for themselves, the vows that were originally made on their behalf by their godparents. There are, however, other ways of doing this. The Methodist 'Covenant Service', for instance – whole congregations, as such, annually renewing their baptismal vows – seems to me an admirable practice. Also, I'm very much in favour of services in which those who, as adults, have returned to Church membership after years out of it would rededicate themselves, with a renewal of their baptismal vows. That might well be made a memorable event.

Or then again – why not a renewal of baptismal vows in the context of a service in which those who've recently retired from work dedicate themselves to a new, more intensive phase in their Church membership? I don't know what such a liturgy would look like. But a dedication-rite for the truly mature, like this, would clearly go far more with the grain of twenty-first-century human nature than the traditional rite of confirmation does. The traditional rite has youngsters making what's theoretically supposed to be a solemn act of commitment to the Church at the very moment in their lives when nature starts to prompt rebellion. Very soon they'll (quite rightly) want to assert their independence from the adults who shepherded them to the altar. And here, of course, is an immediate opportunity for them to do so. All too often in practice the great symbolic act of becoming a full member of the Church has virtually become a passing out parade for teenagers, their moment of departure from the community that they've this very moment joined. Oughtn't we perhaps to take their disappearance as a sort of divine hint? If we were, by contrast, to focus on celebrating the moment in people's lives when they come to retire, however, then we'd be encouraging the very age group most likely to rejoin the Church, or intensify their membership, anyway. And this moreover, in a secular world obsessed with the allure of glamorous youth, would be a prime counter-cultural opportunity to reaffirm the wisdom of age: no shame, no self-pitying regrets!

Why, indeed, as a matter of anthropological fact, has it always seemed so *self-evident* to previous generations that we needed an ecclesiastical initiation rite for young adolescents? Surely, it's all about the internalization of what Paul calls 'law' (not 'grace'). This is the age at which youngsters first begin to become fully capable of internalizing the rules of moral convention, no longer following those rules only out of fear of punishment or hope of reward, but out of inner conviction. Therefore in tribal cultures of every kind the boys especially are put through, sometimes, quite stern tests of pluck and endurance, to mark their transition to the privileges of adulthood. Confirmation is, in effect, a Christian equivalent to such initiation rites. To be sure, it's always been a most half-hearted one – really very feeble by comparison with some! But its basic rationale is the same. I don't observe that, as a rite for young adolescents, it has much serious connection with the asking of the crucial Question. At that age, the crucial Question is nothing but a moody sense of amorphous dismay, intense perhaps, but chaotic. (Again, I'm thinking of my own experience.) It hasn't yet acquired the necessary clear lineaments, the moulding of experience, to be incorporated into truly meaningful liturgy.

And, therefore, the confirmation of young adolescents is no proper celebration of holy *megalothymia*: it's no ritual affirmation of hard-won, God-given individuality. On the contrary, what it's designed to celebrate is nothing other than the polar opposite, the most conventional sort of respectability-code religion, masquerading as 'faith'. It's initiation into the Church-as-tribe.

The whole burden of Paul's urgent message in Romans and Galatians is that faith, true Christian faith, is essentially an experience of liberation from this general species of religion. We mean to honour Paul, the great apostle. Actions, however, speak louder than words. The traditional rite of confirmation evokes a spirit in the Church that, in actual practice, is quite *anti*-Pauline. And it's an intrinsically rather stuffy spirit. By no means all those who preach at confirmation services are pompous or patronizing, but it takes a special talent not to be. The occasion itself so invites it.

People may protest: shouldn't we welcome any opportunity that's given us to communicate the gospel to people in their formative years, so that at any rate they have something, one day, to come back to? Better blank ignorance, I'm inclined to think, than such a trivializing of the matter! The traditional rite of confirmation gives such false prominence to what inevitably tends to be such a very low level of existential understanding. Confirmation training, for adolescents, can't help but tend to convey the message that gospel truth, what the Church most cares about, is very like the content of a school lesson, only without an exam; not something, therefore, to be taken all that seriously.

What are wanted, to supplement the holy *isothymia*, the spirited celebratory affirmation of equality, enacted in infant baptism, are balancing rituals of holy *megalothymia*. That is, a spirited celebratory affirmation and encouragement of each individual's own lifelong pursuit of their individual vocation, as such – an affirmation, in other words, of their quest for wisdom. Not conformity to any conventions of 'law' but to *wisdom*, the sort of wisdom that belongs to the fulfilment of faith, wisdom as an opening to 'grace'. Such wisdom has nothing to do with cleverness. Nor is it a mere accumulation of book learning. Rather, it surely has everything to do with the way one takes to heart the sheer sobering fact of one's *mortality*. It comes from one's appropriating that fact – with calm, but visceral, thoughtfulness – as a stimulus to the asking of the crucial Question. Of course, there may be some 20-year-olds who are wiser than many a 65-year-old, even in this sense. But then those 20-year-olds are liable to be a whole lot wiser yet by the time they reach retirement age. In proposing a rite for the newly retired, I'm not just suggesting that we need liturgically to mark a significant transition in life, as we might also well mark other such transitions, in general. But rather, I'm talking about how the Church is most effectively to celebrate wisdom, as *the* proper goal of faith.

To go back to my initial question in this chapter: what ought the Church to demand of its members? Applying the formula that an ideal Church would be one that was fundamentally dedicated to asking the crucial Question and to nothing else, I think it would forever be saying to them, '*Stop! Think! Why are you here? Sooner or later death will come. And what will your life, then, in the end, have amounted to?*' – just that.

Otherwise, to escape nagging distraction, it needs to make as few demands as possible. But the one thing it must press home continually, and intransigently, with all the poetic resources it can muster, is the simple requirement that we *stop and think*. (Or that we love – but, strictly, in the sense that love is an intensification of soul-shaping thoughtfulness, confronted with mortality.)

How we got to where we are

Let's consider the historical background. I'd love to be able to point back to some golden age in which things were better ordered. But I don't think there ever has been a golden age. We've never had a set of initiation practices clearly and explicitly determined by the demands of an ideal commitment to truth-as-openness, alone. Instead, Church practice in this area has always been a bit of a muddle.

It's actually unclear how far back in Church history the practice of infant baptism goes: whether perhaps already, right from the beginning, when whole households were converted and baptized, the children were also included as a matter of course.[3] Hard evidence only begins to emerge at the beginning of the third century. Tertullian, writing in around the year 200, briefly discusses the matter; it seems infant baptism was a familiar practice at that time, but it's unclear how prevalent. He, at any rate, deplores it. This is because Tertullian is an advocate of what one might call *furious* faith: for him, faith involves a fanatically unflinching confrontation with the pagan world. This is no child's play – far better, he thinks, to keep innocent children out of it. (Tertullian has no notion of original sin, it's clear to him that children *are* innocent.) Many in the persecuted churches of the third century, however, drew different conclusions. These communities felt the need to guarantee their survival by implanting Christian identity, in the most decisive fashion, into the hearts and minds of their children. And to them, infant baptism signalled that intent. Hippolytus of Rome in his *Apostolic Tradition* (originally compiled some time between 200 and 220) clearly accepts the practice. Origen, a little later, firmly advocates it. And then Cyprian of Carthage, in the mid-third century, represents a North African Church order that unequivocally required it, as the norm.

During the fourth century, in contrast, after the conversion of Constantine, as the Roman Empire rapidly became Christianized, that original rationale disappeared. The Church was able to relax. And at first, as a result, infant baptism appears largely to have been abandoned – other than when a child's life was in danger. The commitment involved in baptism was so grave – sins committed afterwards were regarded as so much more grievous than before – that it seemed kinder, or more prudent, to defer it. St Augustine was typical of his contemporaries: born in 354, the son of a devout Christian mother and yet, himself, not baptized until he was 33.

However, in his later years, when he was a bishop, Augustine also, crucially, represents the further shift of opinion that followed. In 410 Rome, for the first time in eight centuries, was overrun and sacked by an invading barbarian army, that of Alaric the Goth. The old secular order was starting to disintegrate. Senior churchmen, observing this, increasingly came to see the Church as the sole future guarantor of civilization itself. Henceforth, infant baptism acquired another compelling rationale: now, as a symbol of the need for civilization-preserving Church order to be fully extended over the whole life of society, that's to say, the life of all its members from the cradle to the grave. Augustine, responding to this new rationale, became, as bishop, a fierce advocate of the practice. Only, he did so on the basis of a quite different sort of argument from mine. Thus, what Augustine sees represented in infant baptism *isn't* the absolutely unconditional sheer generosity of unearned divine love for all. On the contrary, it's the urgent need for rescue from the flames of hell, the eternal punishment with which all the children of Adam are threatened, as they share in the guilty heritage of Adam's primordial sin. Augustine's vindication of infant baptism is developed in the course of his polemic against Pelagianism, in the years 412–15. Against the Pelagians, he argues that infants are as much involved in the guilt of original sin as are adults. The only remedy is through loyal membership within the Church; *therefore*, the sooner they're baptized the better. This argument rests on a punitive notion of divine justice that appears to me fundamentally manipulative. It's very much what I'd call Divine Despot theology.[4]

Meanwhile, as for the linkage between infant baptism and first communion: this, again, has fluctuated. Origen, writing in *c.* 235, makes it clear that in Palestine, and probably also in his native Egypt, there was a certain interval fixed between the two. Cyprian, however, a few years later, indicates that in North Africa all the baptized, including infants, were admitted to communion.[5] And the evidence suggests that it was the North African pattern that, at first, tended to prevail, everywhere, following the general revival of infant baptism in the fifth century.

It's actually in the fifth century, also, that confirmation, as a separate rite from baptism, requiring a bishop, first began to evolve in the West. The earliest use of the Latin term *confirmatio*, with this meaning, and the first attempt to provide a theological rationale for it, are to be found in a Whitsunday sermon by Bishop Faustus of Riez, in southern Gaul, some time around the year 460.[6] What first gave rise to this coming apart of the two rites was the difficulty that bishops had in getting round the remoter regions of their dioceses: one might have to wait years before the bishop was there to perform the confirmation. That there was no such coming apart in the East is basically due to the simple reason that, in the Eastern Church, 'chrismation' didn't have to be performed by a bishop.

At this stage, confirmation *wasn't* regarded as a precondition for communion. In the later mediaeval West generally, though, there then began to develop, again, a renewed tendency for first communion to be delayed, sometimes long after baptism. And in England this tendency was inadvertently accentuated by the initiative of Archbishop John Peckham, in 1281. Peckham, a strict disciplinarian, was concerned that so many parents were neglecting, entirely, to have their children confirmed; the pastoral connection between bishop and people transacted through confirmation was being lost. He it was who therefore, for the first time, made it an official rule that no one from now on should receive communion until they'd been confirmed. For Peckham, this was an attempt to encourage confirmation at a very young age. But then the normal age involved kept on rising. So that when the sixteenth-century Reformers adopted

Peckham's rule it's clear they envisaged confirmation as a rite for school-age children, aged at minimum seven.[7]

Even today, mind you, the Protestant practice of confirmation isn't always dysfunctional. My argument is that it's a fundamental *theological* error to envisage adolescent confirmation as the primary supplement to infant baptism, or the gateway to communion. But, in *sub-theological* terms, the institution, interpreted that way, still does work quite admirably, for instance, in Finland.

Thus, although the general rate of actual churchgoing in Finland is rather low, confirmation remains a rite of passage for around 90 per cent of all 15-year-old Finns each year. Most nowadays join summer confirmation-training camps, in the woods or on the shores of lakes. More than a third of them then go on to participate in the Young Confirmed Voluntary Workers scheme; many 16- and 17-year-olds become group leaders for the confirmation-training camps of the next two cohorts. And the actual confirmation service is a highly charged civil-religious event, for the whole community.

However, its power here clearly lies in its *civil*-religious character. One can't help but think that it's much more about initiation into being Finnish than about initiation into being Christian. Better perhaps than any other, the Finnish Church actually fulfils the purpose that Henry VIII, at the beginning, had in mind for the Church of England: to be the religious agency of national unity. There's much to admire in Finnishness. To my mind, one of the hallmarks of a morally sound political culture is people's willingness, in principle, to pay high taxes. (For isn't tax-paying the chief sacrament of fellow citizenship?) The Finns are happy to pay, by British standards, fantastically high taxes – and furthermore it appears, long term, to have done their economy a power of good. Their willingness to pay high taxes derives from the fact that they feel, it seems, so much more strongly than the British do: '*We're all in this together.*' And that's also what they're affirming when they gather in church for the confirmation of the nation's 15-year-olds. The outcome's enviable. But, despite the Church context, this sentiment of togetherness is surely more a consequence of ethnic homogeneity, and the sharing of a highly idiosyncratic language, than a product of shared Christian faith. Finnish is such a very distinctive, consensual and cosy identity. What we see in the Finnish practice of confirmation is essentially a celebration of the most successful sort of modern tribalism. And, in any case, there's no way that we in our cosmopolitan, multiply fractured culture here in Britain, today, can ever hope to emulate the Finns. We Anglicans need to reinvent ourselves, but *that* isn't a realistic option.

When Henry VIII first decreed the separation of the Church of England from the Church of Rome, with himself as its 'head', what he wanted was, above all, an institution to provide religious back-up to law and order, in the classic mode of 'first modernity'. Confirmation in the Church of England has traditionally been the affirmation of two loyalties in one: loyalty to God and loyalty to the law-and-order establishment. Once upon a time it was a common belief among the propertied classes that, unless the poor were restrained by the fear of hellfire and encouraged by the promise of heaven, the likely outcome would be anarchy. But now we know better! Far more than the fear of hellfire, for this purpose, we simply need an efficient police, and far more than the promise of heaven, the tangible promises of economic growth. So experience has shown us. And, in principle at least, this discovery surely represents a quite delightful opportunity of liberation for the Church. At last, it sets us free from a mighty distraction, which has for far too long held us in thrall.

The dysfunctional nature of the traditional Church of England baptism-and-confirmation regime, in the present context, is plain enough for all to see. For the most part we still haven't thought about it very radically. But the old order's already started to slip: in many parishes, now, Archbishop Peckham's link between confirmation and first communion has, in fact, now been abandoned. The average age of those being confirmed is rising; much younger children are being admitted to communion, even if not, quite yet, immediately from the point of baptism.

What's made this new development, such as it is, possible? In the first place, I take it to be a sign that the Church is tacitly giving up its old law-and-order interests: we're no longer anything like as committed as we once were to instilling the fear of God into adolescents. Nor will they let us. Meanwhile, however, we're altogether more serious than before about providing a real eucharistic welcome to young families, in their entirety. And, of course, it does frustrate us to see newly confirmed adolescents drifting away.

In general, the old forms of English Anglican respectability-code religion are being severely weakened. We still don't want to be a sect; in that sense, we want to stay in the middle of our society. But our response to the brokenness of the middle has changed: instead of seeking to cow conscientious dissent, as we once did, now we're increasingly open to it. Things are moving in the right direction. All that's presently needed is a real *theological* push, as well, to speed the process on.

5

Beyond bishops-as-politicians

'When the Spirit of truth comes . . .'

How then will a Church ideally dedicated to the crucial Question build, as it must, towards a global communion? Let me say at once, I don't think it'll do it the way the Anglican Communion, so far, has.

And yet, I don't think it'll do it in anything like the traditional Roman Catholic way, either. For, again, such a Church will never want to censor ideas, as Rome does. To be sure, it'll see itself as the guardian of rich resources for thinking about ethics and politics, as about everything else – but never as the protagonist of a mandatory party line on particular ethical or political issues. The contribution it'll make to the resolution of the problems that face humanity as a whole will be by trying to help decontaminate the moral atmosphere of public debate, not by throwing its whole official authority behind particular controversial opinions.

I've always been a bit bemused by the distinction people so often draw between questions of public policy that are, supposedly, the proper primary concern of churches, on which political parties are best advised to remain neutral; and vice versa. Of course, I can see how this arrangement (typical of 'second modernity') suits both sides, in that it minimizes the risk of harmful friction, as each backs off from the other's turf. But it seems to me that this renders the Church far too *similar* to political parties. A Church ideally dedicated to the task of channelling the crucial Question, and to nothing else, won't differ from political parties, as regards its approach to public policy, merely by focusing on a different area of primary concern from theirs. Rather, it'll differ in the whole quality of prayerful mutual listening that it brings to its debates, on all matters of concern. As it happens, my own instincts with regard to the chief Roman Catholic 'issues of religious conscience' – abortion, family law, genetic engineering and so forth – are, in any case, somewhat different from those informing official Roman Catholic policy. That, however, isn't the point. I wouldn't want to belong to a Church with an *official line* on these topics, of any kind – not even if that line was in perfect correspondence with my own instincts. Again, I'm also intensely allergic, for instance, to party-political propaganda of the sort that makes great play of a promise to cut taxes, or that seeks to justify the deployment of weapons of mass destruction. Yet, I don't want my church to have an *official line*, even if it was one that I could script myself, on those topics either. It's the Church's job to challenge propaganda thinking, as such, on every side; so far as possible, to inhibit the propagandists; and then to create an ideally open, ideally resonant, space for other, more genuine sorts of thinking. But that's all. To demand that the Church adopt a 'correct' policy, in anything like the way political parties have policies, on any topic outside its own direct jurisdiction, is merely to hamper, by distraction, its proper critique of propaganda.

While, as for questions of internal discipline, how the Church is to organize *itself*: here, I want to argue, let's stick to the one key element of real theological truth underlying the original argument of the sixteenth-century Anglican Reformers.

'When the Spirit of truth comes, he will guide you into all the truth . . .' (John 16.13). How, in general, is such guiding-forward best facilitated? Surely, the Holy Spirit works through human *experiment* – in response, always, to fresh problems, and fresh opportunities, as these open up in the local context.

By its nature, experimentation involves endless error; but truth requires both testing by error, in order to stay alive, and the risk of error, in order to make progress. In principle, we need a Church culture that gives as much room as is practically possible for experiment. Which means providing local churches with plenty of leeway, so that each may pursue its own distinctive path, without interference from outside. Therefore: '*English rules for the English Church!*' the Reformers cried.

The Anglican Reformation was a messy, violent business, largely reflecting the profound corruption of its preceding context. But, as in almost every domestic dispute there are at least some fragments of truth in the argument on both sides, so too here. And that elementary principle, '*English rules for the English Church*', was, I'd argue, the one great truth on the Reformers' side. The trouble, though, is that we've never adequately thought through what it implies, for the construction of a global Anglican Communion. As is, now, only too painfully apparent.

Indigenous rules for each Church independently

'*English rules for the English Church*', not Roman ones: generalizing this sixteenth-century principle, and applying it to the present day, we surely also have to say, '*American rules for the American Church*', '*Nigerian rules for the Nigerian Church*' and so forth. Even if, from the outside, certain Church cultures don't look very appetizing, still, this can *never* justify excommunication, or, therefore, the sort of aggressive intervention in the affairs of another ecclesiastical province that springs from regarding others, hitherto one's partners in communion, as more or less excommunicate. Shouldn't this be accepted as the basic rule of rules, underlying global Anglican identity?

For isn't that rule of rules, in fact, exactly what an ideal channelling of the crucial Question requires: a resolute determination to hold conversation open even with those who are most different from oneself, the sheer difference of whose world-view is most challenging to one's own? And where moral reform is needed, isn't it more likely to be achieved through a holding open of friendly, but critical, conversation than by grand gestures of self-righteous disgust?

Yet, as things are at present, the Anglican world appears, on the contrary, to be full of ecclesiastical warlords simply itching to declare themselves in 'impaired communion' with one another. Local disputes are forever escalating, made occasions for international schism. Feud after feud. And there, in the midst of it all, is Rowan Williams, one of the most gifted Archbishops of Canterbury we've ever had, with a perhaps quixotic, but I think admirable, unflagging appetite for patient mediation, seemingly overwhelmed by hurricanes of bullying malevolence, struggling, sometimes failing, to keep his balance. Observing this tragic spectacle, I can't help thinking that the organizational system of our failed Communion requires far more than just the tinkering reforms currently being introduced.

To be sure, the deep-rootedness of persecutory homophobia in Church tradition is liable to be a problem for the preaching of the gospel under any sort of organizational system. It's so easy to misuse Scripture as justification for it. Fuse this with resentment against the perceived arrogance of Americans, that is, with all the more-or-less inevitable tensions deriving from the USA's superpower status. Add the democratic divisiveness of the Episcopalian Church in the USA, with its well-funded 'conservatives' eager to spread their struggle internationally. Mix in the natural desire of ex-British colonies, especially in Africa, to assert their cultural independence. Of course – what creates the conflict isn't only the bad design of the organizational system. But, clearly, the dysfunctional nature of that system does also contribute to the mayhem. For here we have a great clamour from people demanding, in effect, Roman Catholic levels of official uniformity, and a complete absence of actual mechanisms capable of delivering it.

In principle, we face a stark choice. Either we try and create such mechanisms – so as to become a sort of Protestant tribute act, more or less imitating Rome. Or else we start *unlearning the attitudes that have led to the clamour*. And then we reshape the system, so as to create something much more distinctive: a global order, full of creative energy, that's nevertheless, without any equivocation, based on the broken-middle principle of '*indigenous rules for each Church independently*', in a much more positive and thought-out way than before.

The conservative evangelical Bishop of Nelson, in New Zealand, pungently described the 2008 Lambeth Conference as 'the most expensive exercise in futility that I have ever been to'.[1] It was undeniably expensive: costing about £5 million, and leaving the organizers in very considerable debt. Other people, by contrast to the Bishop of Nelson, considered it a success – inasmuch as, against expectation, 670 Anglican bishops from around the world managed to spend 20 days together, without anyone staging a walkout or any new crises emerging. But then that was largely because the hardcore conservative malcontents, about a quarter of those invited, had, as a matter of principle, declined to come. Some 291 of them having, a month earlier, joined with like-minded clergy and laity for the Global Anglican Future Conference (GAFCON) in Jerusalem, to lay the foundations for a new alternative Anglican Communion, no longer run from Canterbury. Moreover, the 2008 Lambeth Conference made no attempt to pass any resolutions. There was therefore no repetition of the fiasco that had occurred at the end of the preceding, 1998 Conference, when the passing of a resolution on homosexuality had merely served to escalate the conflict, to a calamitous extent. But if Lambeth 2008 could be judged 'successful', this was, in short, only because its organizers were resigned, from the outset, to its being what many would regard as 'futile'.

And the upshot is that now we're left with two rival projects, both attempting to create new mechanisms for an Anglican

Communion with an altogether greater degree of official, policed, global uniformity. On the one hand, GAFCON: making such uniformity much easier to achieve by drastically reducing the level of underlying pluralism within the Communion – with the expulsion, among others, of people like me. On the other hand: the Lambeth-approved process of developing a new 'Covenant' for churches to sign up to, as the basis for a formal system through which provinces may, in future, seek to control, or expel, one another. In my view, however, both projects are wrong-headed. Both, at different degrees of intensity, are symptomatic of the same basic theological error.

The idea of the Covenant was first formally proposed in the Windsor Report of 2004. That report was a response to the crisis resulting from three events in the spring and summer of the previous year.[2] First: the democratic decision of the diocese of New Westminster, on the Canadian west coast, officially to approve church blessings of same-sex partnerships. Second: the non-appointment, following a well-organized international outcry, of a celibate gay man, known to be critical of the 1998 Lambeth Conference resolution on homosexuality, as a suffragan bishop in the Thames Valley. Third: the democratic choice of an openly gay man to be Bishop of New Hampshire, and the failure of protesters, despite another well-organized international outcry, to overturn it. The Covenant proposal was the centrepiece of the report's recommendations. Its aim was to try and head off what in 2008, with GAFCON, actually happened: formal schism within the Communion – look, in its original purpose it's already failed! This failure is the basis of my present hope. I'm hopeful that, in consequence, the time may now have come to open up an altogether fuller reconsideration of the sort of unity that's really wanted.

The bishops at the 2008 Lambeth Conference were presented with a draft of the Covenant to consider. Debate, for the most part, focused on two parts of the document: Section 3.2, setting out the basic principles behind the proposed new process for settling disputes between provinces, and the Appendix, suggesting procedures. Here, though, I'd like to reconsider another passage, one that, so far as I'm aware, none of the gathered bishops, themselves, questioned at all. Namely: paragraph 3.1.3, on the general role of bishops, as such, in relation to Church unity. It runs as follows.

> Each church of the Communion affirms . . . the central role of bishops as guardians and teachers of faith, leaders in mission, and as a visible sign of unity, representing the universal Church to the local, and the local Church to the universal.

How, in actual practice, are bishops meant to fulfil this 'central role' of theirs, to be 'a visible sign of unity'?

It might be thought that the answer's obvious: by meeting together, of course, to exercise appropriate leadership. For that's always been the way of it. And it's clear that this is also what the Covenant intends, since the new system it puts forward presupposes a regular cycle of such meetings. But I'd like to challenge that.

My whole argument, after all, has been that, guided by the lodestar of perfect truth-as-openness, we need to be ready for the possibility of quite new developments in Church practice. Well, here's another example. Thus: the draft Covenant describes bishops as 'guardians and teachers of faith' and as 'leaders in mission'. It's to be hoped they are – and yet the same, at least to some extent, might be said of all other priests, as well. The one thing, in contrast, that's inescapably unique to a bishop, in relation to other priests, is his or her *disciplinary* role. Bishops reward the gifted and the diligent, by virtue of their control over appointments, and they punish clerical miscreants. At the provincial level they participate ex officio in determining the rules that govern the clergy's work; at the diocesan level they're responsible for the day-to-day application of those rules. Whatever else bishops may or may not do, first and foremost surely, in their specific role as bishops, they're the agents of local church discipline. Their various other roles have all got to fit in with that. And so why, then, if we believe in the good old Anglican principle of '*indigenous rules for each Church independently*', should we expect bishops (bishops, of all people!) also to be the leading agents of global Church unity? As agents of discipline their primary role, according to this principle, is strictly diocesan and provincial.

Let's learn the great new lesson of 'third modernity': the global unity we should be looking for surely *isn't* a unity of shared coercive discipline. It's a unity of sharing in free-spirited conversation: the sort of conversation stirred up by, and airing, the crucial Question; with none of the mutual suspicion that's bound to arise as soon as the people of one culture seek to impose their disciplinary will on the people of another culture. Surely, therefore, the very last people to whom we should give the task of opening up global conversation within the Church are the people whose chief responsibility is for discipline. Isn't the recent history of the Anglican Communion, indeed, a terrible cautionary tale, illustrative of what may happen – even in a Church culture the whole original *raison d'être* of which was '*indigenous rules for each Church independently*' – if you do? Really, it isn't surprising when bishops start wanting to discipline one another. No matter how inappropriate their behaviour may be for the international context, they're simply doing what they're used to, back home. *In entrusting this job to our bishops, we were just asking for trouble, right from the outset.*

Bishops, according to the formulation of the draft Covenant, are called to be 'a visible sign of unity, representing the universal Church to the local, and the local Church to the universal'. Liturgically, I think – yes. But only in the same way that a constitutional monarch is understood to be a symbolic focus for national unity. It needs to be a purely symbolic role, with no exercise of actual power involved, at all.

I've perhaps been lucky: all of the bishops I've ever personally got to know I've rather liked as individuals. Some I've very much admired. But still – let's not overload them. They've more than enough to do in their various home contexts. The proper primary agents of global Anglican unity aren't the bishops. There are, surely, *three* basic categories of appropriate 'leaders' in this regard: (1) theologians and, in a broad sense, Christian poets; (2) church-related campaigners for justice and peace; and (3) missionary pioneers and activists. For, what counts, in the end, is the quality of the conversation that's generated by our comings-together; the depth of reflection, the passion of generosity and the freshness of thought that's brought to bear. And aren't these, therefore, the people with the most important contributions to bring to the sort of conversation in question? (The sharp-eyed may also discern an underlying trinitarian rationale to this threefold categorization.) To be sure, there are plenty of bishops who might also be included in each of these three categories. But a theologian, or a church-related campaigner for justice and peace, or a missionary activist who becomes a bishop should, in my view, immediately be *disqualified*, by virtue of that incompatible appointment, from the international councils of the Communion. We need to keep the roles, in the strictest possible fashion, separate. That, I think, is the proper, distinctive logic of Anglican identity. Only so, in the long run, will we be able to escape the sort of chaos into which we've now fallen, without lapsing, GAFCON-style, towards sectarianism.[3]

Officially, there are four 'Instruments of Communion' binding Anglicans together, worldwide:

1 *The Archbishop of Canterbury*. In the global arena, this has become an impossible job – unless the Archbishop is content (which God forbid!) simply to operate as an ecclesiastical warlord among warlords. Otherwise, he's set up from the outset to be a mediator between people many of whom don't in fact want mediation at all, but had much rather try and bully the mediator. The proposed Covenant

would indeed ease things for the Archbishop by *diffusing* the pathological bitterness that's at present channelled towards his office. But diffusing the bitterness is only a palliative remedy. What's needed is a fundamental shift in ethos that would begin to *dispel* that bitterness altogether, by doing away with the false expectations, of disciplinary uniformity, that generate it. And the trouble with the Covenant scheme is that it feeds those very expectations. Any move to ease the pressure by increasing the Archbishop's actual power, in the global arena, must face immediate challenge, because of the way he's appointed: provoking cries – I think they'd be quite justifiable cries – of 'British imperialism'. No doubt it's helpful to have a ceremonial sovereign figure for the purposes of the Communion's relationship with the Vatican and with the Orthodox Churches. It may also make sense for the Archbishop to oversee, in episcopal fashion, appointments to the Communion's central bureaucracy. But, besides such residual roles, what else is needed? There's no lack of domestic English business with which the Archbishop has to deal. I think it would be kinder not to demand more.

2 *The Lambeth Conference.* The first Lambeth Conference in 1867 was a controversial initiative. A number of those invited, including Archbishop William Thomson of York, and most of the other Northern English bishops, declined to come (although Thomson did relent when the second Conference was organized in 1878). And, most remarkably, the liberal-minded Dean Stanley of Westminster Abbey refused to allow the Abbey to be used for the closing service, because of his opposition to the whole enterprise. Many evangelicals were sceptical about the compatibility of such a conference with the original principles of the English Reformation. In retrospect, I think that these sceptics have been proved right.[4] There have now been 14 Lambeth Conferences. It's hard to think of a single thing that any of them has ever

achieved that couldn't have been accomplished in other ways. In 1920 the Lambeth Conference issued an uncompromizing condemnation of all forms of artificial contraception. By 1930 that position was already slipping, and in 1958 it was completely reversed. The Lambeth Conference of 1948, responding to the emergency ordination of Florence Li Tim-Oi during the Japanese occupation of Hong Kong, was unequivocally dismissive of the very idea of women's ordination.[5] In 1968 the issue was reopened; thirty years later there were 11 women bishops actually attending the Conference. But these developments would surely have taken place anyway. The scandalous acrimony of 1998 was unprecedented, but only because previous Lambeth Conferences had been much more firmly held together by the hegemonic spirit of British cultural imperialism. Much of the tension that's now torn the Communion apart derived from people looking forward, either with unseemly anticipation or else with dread, to the prospective crisis of the next Lambeth Conference. It's very much to be hoped that the 2008 Conference will prove to have been the last.

3 *The Primates' Meeting.* Archbishop Donald Coggan originally set this up in 1978, as a regular coming-together of the chief archbishops or bishops of the 38 provinces of the Communion, for 'leisurely thought, prayer and deep consultation'. That, though, might be regarded as a rather charitable description of how it's actually functioned in recent years. The Primates' Meeting appears in fact to have become the most dysfunctional element in the entire system; and all the more so now that GAFCON has established its own Primates' Council. It should be abolished forthwith.

4 *The Anglican Consultative Council* (ACC). Set up in 1968, and meeting every other year, the ACC is a mixed-membership organization. Each of the 10 largest provinces has 3 delegates, a bishop, a priest and a layperson; each of the 10 next largest provinces has 2 delegates, one ordained and one

lay; and each of the 18 smaller provinces plus the Church of Ceylon has a single delegate, preferably a layperson. Delegates are elected for 6-year stints. And then there are a few co-opted members, in addition. In other words, it's the smallest possible entity capable of providing roughly proportionate representation to all of the provinces. The ACC has of course also caught the disease of schismatic dissension afflicting the whole Communion. But there clearly *is* a need for some such advisory council, more or less this size, to initiate, supervise and help fund the international conversation-processes – between theologians, campaigners for justice and peace, and missionary activists – that are, in my view, the Communion's true business. Also, to deal with ecumenical relationships, and relationships with the United Nations and other secular bodies of international governance. If this body didn't have to include bishops, it might well manage to achieve a much better, more representative balance, in its membership, between the genders and between age groups. In an ideal world, I think that its role would very greatly expand.

Let's, as the saying is, go back to basics: why do we have bishops?

Why, in the first place, do we have clergy at all?

The Quakers are in many ways a very good advertisement for doing without. But it's a question of how the community is to preserve its unity. Quakers do so by opting for a certain sort of collective social marginality: they're unified by their shared commitment to rigorous pacifism, and by all that goes with that. So, too, other traditions in which the difference between clergy and laity is minimized are likewise held together by various shades of shared puritanism. In practice, it seems that there are two ways for a Church to hold together: either *pre-structurally*, by a shared option for social marginality, or else *structurally*, by some sort of clerical hierarchy. If, as I do, one wants to belong to a Church that's both coherent and broadly inclusive of all sorts – creating a conversation space in which pacifists and non-pacifists, puritans and non-puritans, are equally welcome – then the evidence suggests that this requires clergy.

And, more particularly, we have bishops because we've opted against a simple free market in clerical leadership. The basic alternative to Church governance by bishops is a system of Church governance by self-appointed, entrepreneurial clergy, who rise to authority by virtue of their sheer charismatic ability to gather a crowd around them. Such a system is certainly liable to produce a much livelier, more flamboyant type of religious culture than that of episcopally led churches. But it comes with rather obvious risks attached: above all, I think, a heightened risk of manipulatively tyrannical leadership and bullying. At least a system of episcopal governance makes it possible for prospective clergy to be vetted in terms of their pastoral sensitivities, and also to be trained accordingly.

Why bishops? Not least, I'd argue that bishops are there, as the chief agents of authority in a diocese, in order to protect local congregations from bullying by clergy, and to protect the clergy from bullying by congregations. And they're there to get the various parishes of the diocese to act as partners in a common enterprise, without the wealthier parishes seeking to bully and dominate the others, by threatening to withhold financial support. Of course, bishops do have many other roles, which may well take up much more actual time. (Indeed, I think it's good if they're disciplinarians with a light touch, also, in their local context.) Again, though, I'm talking about their indispensable *core* role, the one that, more than any other, truly justifies their distinctive authority.

But if bishops, themselves, start to act as bullies, then, clearly, the whole system's failed. It should no doubt, therefore, be the prime criterion in appointing bishops that potential bullies, no matter what their other talents, need to be excluded. And, at the same time, when it comes to devising the structures of Church life, everything ought to be done to minimize the potential rewards of bullying, to those in positions of author- ity. However, the basic failing of our present system within the Anglican Communion is that this system, on the contrary, rewards episcopal bullies. It does so quite gloriously, giving them a global scene in which to grandstand, with nothing to restrain them. If they gang up with certain like-minded colleagues, plotting to bully certain others, they become news- worthy, and receive raucous applause from their partisan follow- ers. The better to do so, moreover, they need to ensure that they've got maximum public support, behind them, in their own provinces and dioceses: another major inducement to bully dissidents there. This is a system that's very liable to corrupt good people. Sincere, devout, otherwise civilized people get caught up into the politics of hatred – the scandal is that our Church order systematically encourages it. There's nothing in the Covenant proposal to turn that basic problem around. We surely do need to be more radical.

A decisive return to the principle of '*indigenous rules for each Church independently*' need not mean any lessening of com- mitment to the global Communion. I'm not advocating that any less money should be spent on building it up. The £5 million spent on the 2008 Lambeth Conference, for instance, might have bought so much more by way of fruitful international contacts and constructive thinking about global Anglican identity if it had been used to fund other sorts of initiative. Such things as: church twinning arrangements and exchanges, international church aid projects, communion-building scholarships, specialist working groups tackling particular issues of common concern. And then add all the money spent on GAFCON, as well – such a quantity of self-indulgent expenditure on an alpha-male feud!

How might things begin to shift away from this? The future that GAFCON represents is one of endless schism. And, by way of another option, all that the Covenant offers is the prospect of a new, increasingly litigious Communion – as the Covenant is, in essence, a framework for litigation. But, now, consider an alternative scenario.

In the future I imagine, at least some bishops – only a few at first, but a steadily increasing number – will begin to break free. They'll make a pledge of constructive restraint. Either at their consecration or later, they'll publicly repeat, and set their signature to, something like this formula:

> As a bishop in the Anglican Communion, treasuring our historic unity-in-difference, and trusting in the Holy Spirit, I [name] hereby pledge entirely to abstain from all contentious meddling in other provinces' affairs. So help me God. Amen.

The title of 'pledging bishop' will become a badge of honour: 'pledging bishop' as opposed to 'schismatic bishop' or 'litigious bishop'. For these pioneers, at least, the Days of Rancour will be over.

Ah, to have done with the Days of Rancour, and to set them, once and for all, behind us, as a monstrous aberration! Gradually, in the future I'm imagining, more and more diocesan synods will also vote that way. Even where bishops aren't directly elected, synods will make it clear that – while, of course, they accept the authority of the bishops they already have – they won't, in future, willingly accept the appointment of 'schismatic' or 'litigious' bishops to their territory, only 'pledging' ones. Grave disagreements will remain, on all sorts of issues, both between provinces, in terms of official policy, and within provinces. Some provinces will continue to follow official policies that I, for my part, regard as abhorrent. And, as I'm not a bishop – and therefore don't speak with the sort of authority that immediately carries with it an implicit threat, sooner or later, of excommunication – I'll feel free to say so, and to support the dissidents in those provinces with my voice. Debate will continue to be vigorous. But the one thing removed will be the poison inherent in the symbolic practice, and the threat, of provinces excommunicating other provinces. A new sense of sin will develop: international conferences of bishops, if they involve communiqués or press conferences, will come to be regarded as, by their very nature, occasions of sin. There'll be no need of a Covenant. After the Days of Rancour, new Days of Listening will thus have begun.

Is this just a fantasy?

The tragic story of St Gregory Nazianzus

Of course, my proposal amounts to a fundamental repudiation of the old imperial Byzantine and Roman traditions, as regards the role of bishops. But right from the outset, surely, those traditions were all too imperial.

The Christian gospel originated as a great symbolic onslaught against the governing ethos of the Roman Empire, the agency of crucifixion. Although the persecution that the early Church suffered was haphazard, there was nothing arbitrary about it. Yet, when, in the early fourth century, the persecution ceased, and Christianity swiftly became the dominant religious culture throughout the Empire, the imperial ethos gained its great revenge: it penetrated the organization of the Church itself. And one of the prime symptoms of this was the transformation in the role of bishops. They became, in status, not unlike ecclesiastical equivalents to imperial governors, like Pontius Pilate. Emperors, from Constantine onwards, looked to the bishops to help preserve the unity of the Empire. So they summoned ecumenical councils, gathering the bishops together for that essentially secular paramount purpose.

I think we'd do well to ponder, in relation to our present plight, the testimony of one of the truly great saints of early Byzantium: *St Gregory of Nazianzus* (?329–90). For Gregory was a man fundamentally persuaded of the radical conflict, in principle, between the true ethos of the gospel, promoting humility, and the false ethos of Empire, promoting love of power. Nevertheless, he dutifully took his place in the 'broken middle' of his world and then, in his grief-filled verse autobiography, painted his own vivid picture of the conflict, as he'd personally lived it.[6]

Gregory was a man with a clear calling to help advance the cause of Orthodox Christian unity. The son of a bishop, he was perhaps the greatest literary figure of his age, a gifted orator, a bold theologian. His tragedy was that, in that culture, people like him were automatically expected, also, to become bishops. Which, however, meant entanglement in all sorts of worldly prestige struggles, since bishops now had, like it or not, become such major politicians. He recoiled from this. His original idea was to live as a lay Christian philosopher. It was his father who 'forced' him, he says, to accept ordination – he calls it a 'terrible shock'.[7] And it was his beloved friend, Basil, bishop of Caesarea, who later ensured that he was made bishop. Basil, a wily political operator engaged in bitter struggle against the Arian bishop of Tyana, needed a reliable ally as bishop of the newly created little diocese of Sasima. Gregory gave way, was consecrated, but never took up the post – such was the Arian opposition, he says, that he couldn't have done so without bloodshed. Moreover, he felt used and betrayed by Basil. Even in this case, he comments,

> Souls were the pretext, but the real cause was desire for power.
> I hesitate to say it, but the wretched fact is that it is revenues and taxes that motivate the whole world.[8]

After a spell of monastic retreat, family loyalty impelled him to work instead, first as an assistant to his father in Nazianzus, and then, after his father's death, as acting bishop there, until someone else might be appointed. But only briefly – for when his colleagues refused to appoint anyone to replace him, again he fled to a monastery.

In 379, lured out of retirement by admiring fellow bishops, Gregory went to work as pastor to the little remnant of Orthodox (that is, Nicene) Christians in what had become the predominantly Arian city of Constantinople. At first he didn't even have a proper church building as his base. Yet, his arrival coincided with the rise to power of the Emperor Theodosius: an Orthodox Emperor, after a series of Arian ones. And suddenly everything changed. In 380 Theodosius returned to Constantinople, expelled the Arian bishop, and designated Gregory as bishop and patriarch in his place.

The following year Theodosius summoned together the bishops of the Eastern Empire, for what later came to be known as the Second Ecumenical Council, the Council of Constantinople. One might think that this would have been a tremendous moment of triumph for Gregory. But, in fact, he experienced it as a searing nightmare. The Egyptian bishops, especially, were hostile: having sought to install their own candidate as bishop of Constantinople, they wanted Gregory deposed. There was also a schism dividing the Orthodox Church at Antioch, with Rome and Alexandria on one side and the rest of the east on the other. Gregory's initial attempts at mediation failed – everywhere he saw faction, back stabbing, and rampant egoism. He resigned.

Gregory's poem 'Concerning his own life', which culminates in this event, is full of self-pity. However, he's frank about his own failings. And the self-pity here isn't only self-indulgent. Rather, it becomes a vehicle for the most trenchant prophetic critique of (what he saw as) a fundamentally corrupted Church. This, for instance, is how he describes himself, anticipating the Council and deciding, despite all his misgivings, to accept the Emperor's appointment:

The vain illusions of my mind led me to think
(for a wish is quick to hope
and all things are easy when the spirit is bubbling with
    eagerness;
I tend anyway to be over-optimistic in such matters)
that if I were to accept the power of the bishop's throne
(for outward appearances are also very influential)
I might be like a chorus-leader between two choruses . . .
as in a dance I would be able to bring together,
some from one side, some from another, those who were
    dreadfully divided.[9]

But what, then, was the actual response to his speech, attempting to resolve the Antiochene schism, at the Council? The assembled crowd, he tells us,

    screeched on every side,
a flock of jackdaws all intent on one thing,
a mob of wild young men, a new kind of gang,
a whirlwind causing the dust to swirl as the winds went out
    of control . . .
buzzing around as they were in complete disorder,
like a swarm of wasps suddenly flying into your face.
Yet the respected council of elders, far from attempting to
    recall
the young men to their senses, actually joined them![10]

From that moment he made up his mind, like an innocent Jonah, as he puts it, to let himself be thrown overboard.[11]

Some years later, in a letter to Bishop Theodore of Tyana, declining to attend a provincial synod, he remarks,

Synods and councils I prefer to salute from a distance. For experience has taught me that, to put it mildly, they're mostly pretty wretched affairs.[12]

Gregory's self-pity is an index of his frustration: in his day he could see no realistic alternative to a Church order unified by the domination of worldly-wise politician bishops. *We* may well be thankful to live in a world so full of different possibilities.

Holy St Gregory, pray for us!

'Two cities' created by opposing 'loves'

Worldly-wise politician bishops behave as though the Church in general, and their own branch of it in particular, existed only to promote itself. They seem to think that true success, for a Church, is measurable by the sheer noise it makes in the public realm. The alternative view is that it exists to promote the kingdom of God, or what Gregory's younger contemporary, St Augustine, thinking of the heavenly Jerusalem in Revelation 21—22, called the 'Heavenly City', as opposed to the 'earthly city'.

Augustine famously defines these 'cities' as the creations of two opposing species of 'love':

> The earthly city was created by self-love reaching the point
> of contempt for God, the Heavenly City by the love of God
> carried as far as contempt of self.[13]

Let's try and be a little more exact, though. The sort of solidarity the Church exists to promote is surely that which is generated by a love for God-*as-Questioner*, forever amplifying the crucial Question. And the defining feature of the 'earthly city', therefore – as the opposite of this – is that it includes everything tending, on the contrary, to close that Question down.

The 'earthly city', thus, includes every form of human co-existence insofar as it's dominated by the sheer inertia of wilful, rigid prejudice. It includes everything generated by fear, reinforcing such prejudice: whether it's panicky fear of disorder, fear of the unruly young, or fear of the outsider – any sort of fear-tainted patriotic sentiment or tribalism. And it includes all that's created by manipulative privilege hunting: the ambitions of the rich and powerful, or, altogether more insidiously, the prestige-claims of the better educated, and of those with particular emotional skills. For manipulation, as it plays upon prejudice, also reinforces it.

Mind you, Augustine is also interested in criticizing the ethos of secularity even at its most genuinely attractive. In the first place, he values the civilizing influence of Roman power. Nevertheless, he argues that the typical 'love of glory' by which its pioneers were driven is still a weaker motivation for civic virtue than true love of God.[14] And, second, 'love of glory' in another form largely inspired the wisdom of the pagan philosophers, for whom he has considerable respect. However, he insists that, as a source of wisdom, love of God is more reliable.[15] Both arguments are surely true – *if by 'love of God' we do indeed mean love for God-as-Questioner, and if, by contrast, 'love of glory' means wanting to be admired by the prejudiced, as such.* For 'love of glory', in that sense, can only motivate virtue insofar as established prejudice itself is virtuous, which it never altogether is.

Yet, there remains, in my view, one little problem with Augustine's own doctrine of the two 'cities'. It's blunted, by being *over-partisan.* So he criticizes the 'earthly city' in its pagan forms and he criticizes forms of Christianity that, he considers, fail to be distinct enough from a pagan ethos. (This is his basic complaint against Pelagianism: the Pelagians have, in effect, reduced Christian virtue to the same level as pagan philosophic virtue. They haven't adequately renounced glory, for themselves, in acknowledging their dependence on divine grace.) But he doesn't seem to see the potential intrusion of 'love of glory' – in the sense of a falling away from the crucial Question – also into quite un-Pelagian forms of orthodox Christian sincerity. As I've said, he's still insufficiently alert to the dangers posed by orthodox Christian forms of love for God-*as-Divine-Despot.*[16]

Going beyond Augustine, therefore, I want to argue that, truly, the *one-and-only* sign of the Heavenly City's presence is the prejudice-dissolving energy of the crucial Question at work.

Again: good theology isn't in the first instance a matter of upholding 'correct' Christian answers to metaphysical puzzles and moral dilemmas. Instead, it's all about devising strategy to cultivate the sort of open, engagingly pluralistic, not elitist but many-layered, tradition-rich, propaganda-free, imaginative, patient and prayerful, soul-shaping public conversation within which the crucial Question best flourishes. Everything else – truly, *everything* else – is collusion with the 'earthly city'.

Other forms of piety may be perfectly orthodox. And they may also be passionately sincere. But look – that isn't enough.

Notes

1 Beyond dogma

1 Richard Dawkins, *The God Delusion* (London: Black Swan, 2007), p. 80.

2 Leo Tolstoy, *War and Peace*, trans. Rosemary Edmonds (Harmondsworth: Penguin, 1978), pp. 338–9, 341.

3 Elsewhere I've used the phrase 'truth-as-Honesty', distinguishing Honesty with a capital 'H', being truly open towards the challenge of what other people have to say, from honesty in the sense of sincerity, truly meaning what one says oneself, or candour, truly saying what one thinks. See Andrew Shanks, *Faith in Honesty* (Aldershot: Ashgate, 2005).

4 Dawkins, *God Delusion*, p. 232.

5 See Wilfred Cantwell Smith, *Faith and Belief* (Princeton, NJ: Princeton University Press, 1979).

6 'The proposition that God exists is *not even* a theory': so Dawkins's American ally Daniel Dennett, in his book *Breaking the Spell: Religion as a Natural Phenomenon* (Harmondsworth: Penguin, 2006), p. 311. Only remove the word 'even', and yes, I agree: the proposition that God exists isn't just a theory.

7 Dawkins, *God Delusion*, pp. 78–9.

8 Dawkins, *God Delusion*, p. 184.

9 Søren Kierkegaard, *Concluding Unscientific Postscript*, trans. Howard V. Hong and Edna H. Hong, in *Kierkegaard's Writings* (Princeton, NJ: Princeton University Press, 1992), vol. 12, part 2, pp. 186–7.

10 Gillian Rose, *The Broken Middle* (Oxford: Blackwell, 1992); and see also Andrew Shanks, *Against Innocence: Gillian Rose's Reception and Gift of Faith* (London: SCM Press, 2008).

11 Dennett, *Breaking the Spell*, p. 222.

12 Dawkins, *God Delusion*, p. 15.

2 'Beyond good and evil'

1 The 'solidarity of the shaken' is a theme I've discussed in numerous places. For what follows, see particularly Andrew Shanks, *The Other Calling: Theology, Intellectual Vocation and Truth* (Oxford: Blackwell, 2007).

2 English translation by Maxwell Staniforth in *Early Christian Writings* (Harmondsworth: Penguin, 1968), p. 121; although Staniforth actually renders *katholikē* here as 'world-wide'.

3 J. H. Newman, letter to H. J. Rose, 10 April 1836 (John Henry Newman, *Letters and Diaries*, Vol. 5, ed. T. Gornall [Oxford: Clarendon Press, 1981]).

4 Polish patriotism is closely identified with the Roman Catholic Church for the simple reason of the contrast with Russian Orthodoxy to the East and with German Lutheranism to the West; it's all the more intense because of the Poles' historic experience of being subject to Russian and German rule. Compare the Czechs: also a majority Roman Catholic people, and ethnically close kin to the Poles, yet, by contrast, one of the *least* religiously observant peoples in Europe. This is because Roman Catholicism was violently re-imposed on the Czechs by their Austrian overlords, in the seventeenth century, after the Czech lands had earlier been home to the earliest form of popular Protestantism, the Hussite movement. As a result of which, there has never been a natural fit between Czech patriotism and Czech Roman Catholicism.

5 Andrew Shanks, *God and Modernity* (London: Routledge, 2000).

6 Jean-François Lyotard, *The Postmodern Condition: A Report on Knowledge*, trans. Geoff Bennington and Brian Massumi (Minneapolis, MN: University of Minnesota Press, 1984), Introduction.

7 Jan Patočka, *Heretical Essays in the Philosophy of History*, trans. Erazim Kohák, ed. James Dodd (Chicago, IL: Open Court, 1996).

8 Francis Fukuyama, *The End of History and the Last Man* (London: Penguin, 1992).

9 Fukuyama develops the earlier, somewhat whimsical argument of Alexandre Kojève. By contrast, Kojève's response to the great established fact of Communism is more equivocal.

3 Beyond Liberal Theology

1 Richard Dawkins, *The God Delusion* (London: Black Swan, 2007), p. 55.

2 By way of remedy for Dawkins's inability, specifically, to make head or tail of the dogma of the Trinity, let me recommend my book, *Faith in Honesty* (Aldershot: Ashgate, 2005).

3 See for example Cupitt's development of his argument in this regard: *Jesus and Philosophy* (London: SCM Press, 2009).

4 D. F. Strauss, *The Life of Jesus Critically Examined* (1835), trans. George Eliot (1846), ed. Peter C. Hodgson (London: SCM Press, 1973).

5 For a comprehensive view of Baur in his historical context, see Horton Harris, *The Tübingen School* (Oxford: Oxford University Press, 1975). Also: Peter C. Hodgson, *The Formation of Historical Theology: A Study of Ferdinand Christian Baur* (New York: Harper & Row, 1966).

6 See Harris, *Tübingen School*, pp. 256–62.

7 Notoriously, a major problem with Hegel is that he's unreadable. The original texts on the 'Unhappy Consciousness' are in his *Phenomenology of Spirit*, trans. A. V. Miller (Oxford: Oxford University Press, 1977), pp. 126–38, 454–7. But one needs a commentary. I made a first stab at interpreting these passages in my (admittedly, *otherwise* not very good) *Hegel's Political Theology* (Cambridge: Cambridge University Press, 1991), Chapter 1. And I've also discussed them, in another context, in *The Other Calling* (Oxford: Blackwell, 2007), Chapter 10.

8 Schleiermacher was indeed, like Hegel, a good liberal in his politics as in his religion: in favour of free speech, consultative government, reining in aristocratic privilege. But when it came to the struggle, in the period following the Napoleonic Wars, between the increasingly illiberal Prussian government and the largely proto-fascist student fraternities (the *Burschenschaften*), he was much more inclined to sympathize with the latter than Hegel was. He was a preacher, a mellifluous orator, intent on transmitting a warm glow of devout feeling to his congregation. Hegel wasn't. In general, Hegel was a caustic character, who rather loathed what he saw as sentimentality, of any kind. They quarrelled bitterly, pretty well from the moment that Hegel arrived in Berlin,

in 1818. See Terry Pinkard, *Hegel: A Biography* (Cambridge: Cambridge University Press, 2000).

9 Dom Gregory Dix, *The Shape of the Liturgy* (London: Dacre Press, A. & C. Black, 1945), p. 744.

4 Beyond baptism-and-confirmation

1 These terms, *isothymia* and *megalothymia*, are the original coinage of Francis Fukuyama, in *The End of History and the Last Man* (London: Hamilton, 1992). The prefix *iso-* means 'equal-'; *megalo-* means 'big-'. *Thymos* may perhaps best be translated as 'spiritedness', with connotations of courage and self-esteem. In the *Republic* 435c–441c, Plato discusses *thymos* as one of the three basic constituents of the soul, alongside reason and desire: it's other than pure reason by virtue of its emotional fieriness, but it's also other than simple desire in that it's bound up with a moral self-image.

Although I'm using the terms in a very positive sense here, it should perhaps be noted that *isothymia* and *megalothymia* are, in themselves, quite morally ambivalent categories. For *thymos* isn't only a form of energy in the service of truth; it's also the natural element of all forms of idolatry, as such. (Idolatry of *isothymia*: the passions of the herd, governed by herd-morality. Idolatry of *megalothymia*: the passions of the tyrant, and of the tyrant's allies, who govern the herd.) In short, it's a name for that whole troubled aspect of the human soul which true religion seeks to redeem and purify.

2 Evelyn Underhill, *Mysticism* (Oxford: Oneworld, 1993 [1911]).

3 The evidence regarding the prevalence, or otherwise, of infant baptism in the first two centuries and the subsequent development of the practice is thoroughly aired in the 1958–63 interchange between the two German scholars Joachim Jeremias and Kurt Aland. Jeremias argues that it was probably widespread from very early on, but Aland disputes this. See Joachim Jeremias, *Infant Baptism in the First Four Centuries*, trans. David Cairns (Philadelphia, PA: Westminster, 1960), and *The Origins of Infant Baptism: A Further Reply to Kurt Aland*, trans. Dorothea M. Barton (Naperville, IL: Allenson, 1963); Kurt Aland, *Did the Early Church Baptize Infants?*, trans. G. R. Beasley-Murray (Philadelphia, PA: Westminster, 1963). For a more recent historical survey of the whole

history of infant baptism, see David Wright, *What Has Infant Baptism Done to Baptism?* (Carlisle: Paternoster Press, 2005).

4 Among earlier theologians arguing in favour of infant baptism, Origen and Cyprian both, more or less, anticipate Augustine's approach. The classic early expression of an alternative approach, not seeing infant baptism as a remedy for original sin at all, but nevertheless affirming it as a symbol of God's covenant with the whole Christian family, is in fact John Chrysostom's, in his *Baptismal Instruction* (trans. Paul W. Harkins [Mahwah, NJ: Paulist Press, 1963]).

Meanwhile, I've also discussed the Pelagian controversy (arguing against both sides alike) in *Faith in Honesty* (Aldershot: Ashgate, 2005), pp. 121–5.

5 Origen, *Homilies on Judges*, trans. Elizabeth Ann Dively Lauro (Washington, DC: Catholic University of America, 2009), 6.2; Cyprian, *On the Lapsed*, trans. Maurice Bevenot (Mahwah, NJ: Paulist Press, 1957), 9. 25.

6 Faustus' basic argument is that baptism remits the guilt of original sin, but confirmation symbolically re-enacts the outpouring of the Holy Spirit at Pentecost.

7 Queen Elizabeth I was an exception: as there was a bishop present, she was both baptized and confirmed at birth. Peckham would have approved. However, this was before the new order had fully settled in.

5 Beyond bishops-as-politicians

1 *Daily Telegraph* (3 August 2008).

2 For a detailed journalistic account of the crisis, written at the same time as the Windsor Report, see Stephen Bates, *A Church at War: Anglicans and Homosexuality* (London: I. B. Tauris, 2004).

3 It's been put to me that perhaps another alternative would be for bishops to give up their disciplinary role altogether, and hand that over to archdeacons.

Well yes, if 'bishop' were nothing more than an honorific title accorded to certain theologians, activists for justice and peace, and missionaries – completely without any associated roles, whatever, in the actual administration of Church affairs, or in the making of clerical appointments – then that would indeed be different!

Of course I'd have no objection to *such* 'bishops' being global players. However, let's be clear: they really would be 'bishops' quite unlike any others that have ever existed, and the new role of 'archdeacon' really would be unrecognizably different from that of any archdeacon hitherto.

4 Much of the actual discussion at the first Lambeth Conference was prompted by the furious campaign, headed by Archbishop Robert Gray of Cape Town, to have John Colenso, Bishop of Natal, internationally condemned as a heretic. It's a relief that he failed to get his way. A major part of Colenso's offence was his 1861 commentary on Paul's Letter to the Romans, in the light of his own mission among the Zulus: a fine, pioneering work of anti-racist theology. By present-day standards, he also held very moderately liberal views on biblical hermeneutics, scandalous to some people. Looking back now, Colenso seems one of the most admirable figures in the, for the most part, quite dire intellectual world of the Victorian Church. See Jonathan Draper (ed.), *The Eye of the Storm: Bishop John William Colenso and the Crisis of Biblical Interpretation* (London: T&T Clark, 2003).

5 Florence Li Tim-Oi had been working as a deacon in Macao, the Church's only minister there, and the occupation had made it impossible for any priests to get through to Macao. Bishop Hall of Hong Kong had therefore, in 1944, ordained her priest in order that the refugee Church community in Macao shouldn't be deprived of the sacraments. See Ted Harrison, *Much Beloved Daughter* (London: Darton, Longman and Todd, 1985).

6 For a more detailed study, see John McGuckin, *St Gregory of Nazianzus: An Intellectual Biography* (Crestwood, NY: St Vladimir's Seminary Press, 2001).

7 Gregory of Nazianzus, 'Concerning his own life', lines 337–40, in *Gregory of Nazianzus: Autobiographical Poems*, ed. and trans. Carolinne White (Cambridge: Cambridge University Press, 1996). Reproduced with permission.

8 Gregory of Nazianzus, 'Concerning his own life', lines 460–2.

9 Gregory of Nazianzus, 'Concerning his own life', lines 1529–35, 1537–8.

10 Gregory of Nazianzus, 'Concerning his own life', lines 1680–3, 1686–9.

11 In the words of his subsequent resignation speech (Gregory of Nazianzus, 'Concerning his own life', lines 1841–3): 'Take me and throw me according to the casting of the lot. / A kindly whale from out of the deep will receive me. / From then on you can start to agree.'

12 Gregory of Nazianzus, Letter 124 (my translation).

13 Augustine, *City of God*, trans. Henry Bettenson (Harmondsworth: Penguin, 1972), XIV, 28, p. 593.

14 Augustine, *City of God*, V, 12–20, pp. 196–215.

15 The particular philosophers, as such, with whom Augustine argues most directly are the Neo-Platonists, above all Porphyry. The one thing holding them back from Christian faith, he suggests, is their pride, and the intrinsic offence of the gospel to all pride: Augustine, *City of God*, X, 29, pp. 414–17.

16 See above: p. 81 (and compare pp. 59–62).

Index

Index